P9-CKH-264

Rocky Fire

The Life Story of an American Quarter Horse

Written and Illustrated by

Marilyn J. Wiley

Wiley Publishing
Kirkland, Arizona

Copyright 2012 by Marilyn J. Wiley
SECOND PRINTING 2016

Cover Photograph by Maggie Bryce

ISBN-13: 978-1539097235
ISBN-10:1539097234

Printed in the United States

Published by:
Wiley Publishing
9424 S. Steven Trail
Kirkland, AZ 86332

All rights reserved. No part of this book may be reproduced or transmitted in any form or by any means, electronic or mechanical, including photocopying, recording, or by any information storage and retrieval system, except as may be permitted by the 1976 Copyright Act or in writing by the author.

This Book is Dedicated to:

Dale Girdner

Books By Marilyn J. Wiley

Rocky Fire
Buffalo Chips and Co.

PART ONE

THE BEST OF TIMES

The mare turned slowly in a circle, her lowered muzzle barely brushing along the tips of the grass beneath her. She circled clockwise twice then buckled her knees and lowered her over sized body to the ground. As her huge belly made contact with the hard surface a muffled 'humph' sound arose into the crisp night air. In the distance other horses quietly grazed, their presence known only to the mare by the sound of grass being torn and their quiet chewing. It was so dark that the outlines of their bodies could not be discerned from the blackness of the night. There was no moon. Above the mare millions of stars cast off their tiny pinpricks of light against that infinite ebony celestial sea that stretched from one horizon to the other.

A night bird warbled an unanswered call. The mare groaned. She stretched herself out flat against the ground. Dried grasses and small rocks poked into her tender hide. Her flanks had started to dampen with sweat. A moment later she rolled herself back up to a more comfortable position but her pain continued. With great effort she heaved herself up again and stood, trying desperately to find relief from the unending pressure. Milk streamed from her swollen udder onto her legs adding to the dried droplets from earlier that afternoon. Unexpectedly a spasm coupled her hindquarters beneath her. It was all she could do to stand. A few seconds later she relaxed and straightened. Her unborn foal was working its way into the world. Circling again, nose to the ground, she sought a place free from the larger rocks and onto the earth she collapsed again. As she stretched her dark body along the ground an object appeared below her tail. The front foot of her foal had reached out to embrace the world. The mare lay flat. She stiffened and emitted a short groan. The tiny dark legs protruding beneath her black tail grew longer. They were wrapped in a rubbery gray bubble. With another grunt from the mare a small muzzle appeared on top of the two front legs. The mare kicked and rolled onto her back and then lay still again. Minutes passed. She breathed heavily. With another heave she expelled the head and then rested again. Within a minute she went back to work and with a long straining effort the foal's shoulders popped through. As they did the gray bubble tore away from the tiny hooves and snapped back across the foal's head almost to his eyes.

The first breath of life entered into his lungs and with his first exhale a tiny sound was heard. Not a nicker, but still a noise which his mother immediately responded to with a soft call of her own. His head flopped about and jerked this way and that. The long dark spindly objects in front of him started working back and forth. Then, like a wave he rode the final separation from his mother in a sudden rush of fluid onto the remote canyon floor.

Far away from any city lights the little brown foal lay in utter darkness. The large dark shape that lay next to him beckoned. He still was not aware of what that mass of warmth was, but instinct told him that he needed to get as close to it as possible. At first he willed himself towards it, as if throwing his head up and down would accomplish the feat. In a moment the realization came to him that the four long objects spread in all directions about him could be controlled somewhat and he set himself diligently upon the task of putting them to work. One front leg was already stretched forward. He threw the other leg towards it but overshot the target and ended up with both legs crossed just about the time his rear legs shoved him forward. Sliding across the ground the newborn foal gained a few inches toward his goal.

He tried again. This time he managed a sitting position before the props pushed him backward into a heap. He lay flat, thinking, then he tried again. After several attempts and failures he finally stood shakily on all four legs, each one braced in an opposite direction. As he nickered the triumph of his first success his mother stood up and as she did so, slightly bumped him. It was enough to send him tumbling back down to the earth. As if to apologize, the giant dark mass turned and touched him with her muzzle then licked his neck. The foal bounced awkwardly back to a quivering standing position. The mare nickered softly and moved her body in close.

Minutes passed. Carefully and very stiff legged, the foal took a step. It was almost his undoing. Had it not been for the body of his mother next to him he would have fallen again. The foal softly bobbed his head along his mother's body. He took another step. The scent of something nearby beckoned to him and he began to search for the source. He wasn't sure what he was looking for but all his focus was centered upon it. He opened and closed his mouth in his search across his mother's side and down her leg. The mare turned her head and licked his rump. It startled the foal so much that he jumped forward almost losing his balance. Once again the mare's body came between the foal and a fall. Regaining his balance he started his search again. This time he followed the scent under his mothers flank and felt a tiny stream of milk spray across his face. Opening and closing his mouth he finally found a nipple to wrap his tongue around, licking then sucking the nectar from his mother.

The mare lifted her hind leg slightly up and to the side. This was her first born. She tried to get her mind around the feeling of pain and relief happening at the same time. Her instinct had sealed the bond to the wobbling foal beside her. His scent was settled deep into her brain. As of yet there was no threat to engage her protective behavior. She was immersed in her curiosity of the newborn nursing beneath her. He pulled away from her nipple and stood leaning against her body, then took a step and then two. He managed to wobble awkwardly around her tail to the other side. The mare stepped forward and the foal followed. His feet were uncertain and he lost his balance on the rough surface of the rocky pasture. He lay on the ground again with his mother standing over him. The next time he stood up his legs were less unpredictable. It was a few moments before he found the teat but now he knew what he searched for. He drank again and then exhausted, collapsed his body into a heap on the ground and fell asleep.

When he awoke the sky in the east had a faint light to it. He could see the shadow that was his mother standing exactly where she had been when he had laid down. He nickered and she softly answered. Excitedly he scrambled to his full height and eagerly went to the source of his delight. As he drank the sky lightened a tiny bit more. He could make out the terrain a few feet around him in all directions. His mother took a step and then walked a few feet. The foal stood for a moment and nickered in protest. When she replied with a soft nicker, the call drew him to her and they walked together, her new foal leaning against her side as they went. The smell of the place of birth would soon reach the noses of coyotes or other predators and she knew she needed to move her foal to a safer location.

The sky lightened as the pair walked up to the wide grassy area above them. The mare stopped to graze and the foal drank again. By then the sky had turned a pale gray. The mare pricked her ears and turned her head back towards the direction they had just come from. She heard the yipping of the coyotes announcing their happy discovery of the left-overs from the recent birth. Her foal had fallen asleep again at her feet. Instinctively she placed her body between him and the unseen predators far below. She touched him with her nose for reassurance. It wasn't long before her new baby awoke and got back to his feet. She quickly inter-rupted his meal and led him further up the slope following the scent of the other mares that had passed along the same trail a few hours earlier. The foal bucked in defiance as his mother walked away. The legs that were so rubbery just a few hours earlier had grown strong. He trotted to catch up to his mother then galloped passed her and stopped. Just as they approached the top of the hill she began grazing again. The other mares were on the far side just out of sight. The foal then returned and immediately began to nurse, then satisfied, lay down to sleep through his first sunrise.

The morning sun warmed the foals brown coat as he lay flat out against the ground. A fly tickled his ear causing it to flinch in his slumber. The warmed earth was giving forth its spring aroma of filaree blossoms, new grass, and dirt dampened with the morning dew. The foal yawned, blinking his eyes as he lifted his head. His mother was standing in front of him looking to the west. He nickered and scrambled to his feet. His focus was on his meal and not what had caught his mother's attention. The other mares had moved further down the west slope of the hill. She let the foal finish a quick meal then began her walk to the west.

As they crested the hill she hesitated. Her mixed feelings made her want to return to the herd and yet at the same time she was concerned for the safety of her foal. Below them just a few hundred yards away was a sorrel mare. The sorrel lifted her head and turned towards the new mother the moment they came within view. In unison the other five mares in the herd took notice and they too followed her gaze back up the hill. Several of them whinnied. The two closest mares moved up the hill to inspect the new foal. As a black mare trotted towards them the new mother laid her ears flat back against her head and pushed the foal behind her. She then lowered her head and curled her lips, swishing her tail violently. Her aggressive action was enough to stop the black mare several yards away. Curiously and from a safe distance the intruder inspected the bay mare and the new foal hidden behind her. The sorrel mare walked up beside the black and also stopped. She too inspected the newborn standing behind the bay mare. The black mare tossed her head. The sorrel mare reached down to graze. Then they both turned back toward the other mares and grazed their way back to the herd. The new mother grazed along behind them with her foal close by her side, accepted back into the herd.

One by one as the morning progressed the mares in the herd acknowledged the new mother and her foal. None came close enough to touch noses with either the new foal or his mother. They respected her space and knew that an intrusion would lead to rebuke in a painful way.

Below the little band of mares the land slowly fell away to the west. In the distance the painted red and white buildings of the ranch headquarters could be seen. Beyond them was a line of giant cottonwood trees that separated the ranch from the two-lane blacktop road known as Highway 89.

The day that bay foal was born I was nearly four hundred miles away. It was a Saturday. That morning I went with my dad to the dairy where he worked in Chino, California. I was oblivious to the fact that something had happened in the mountains of central Arizona that would forever change my life. It would be three and a half years before the foal that was born that morning and I would meet.

Today I would spend the morning helping my dad feed the Holstein cows at the dairy where he worked as a herdsman. As soon as we arrived dad hooked the Ford tractor to a trailer loaded with heavy bales of alfalfa hay. Six hundred hungry mouths awaited their meals on wheels. Although I was only 13 years old, it was my job to drive the tractor. I puttered along at a snail's pace down the concrete lane in front of the corrals as Dad threw off a bale of hay every few yards. Feeding the cattle took over an hour. After the bales were dropped my dad would walk back and cut the three wires away from each and then return with the tractor to spread the hay around with the tractor's bucket.

Other than helping dad feed, my chores were few. Occasionally a heifer needed help delivering her calf and I would be dad's gopher while he was busy with his arm up a cow's rear end. When my chores were finished I spent the remainder of the day climbing through the immense haystacks looking for the mother cat's new kittens or watching the baby calves. My cherished destination on the forty-acre dairy was right in the middle. There in the center was a musty, usually vacant two-stall horse barn. Every so often one of the dairy owner's Quarter Horse broodmares would spend time there. My favorite was a young mare named Royal Pleasure. Her name and the name of her sire and dam were on a brass plate attached to her leather halter. She was the daughter of Royal Bar, a Quarter Horse son of Three Bars. Her dam was Bold Bev, a daughter of Bold Ruler. I loved to brush her and comb out her black mane and tail. For me just being able to be close to a horse was ecstasy. It was always the highlight of my day.

My experience with horses began when I was four years old. At the dairy where we lived the owners cousin put me up on her old gray gelding and led me around the corral. That event lit a fire in me that could not be quenched. I believe God hard-wires different talents into each of us. Some people have an aptitude for sports, flying, math, writing, painting, gardening, teaching, music, etc. The list goes and on and on. We are all gifted in an innumerable swath of skills and interests. For me, I was destined to be a horse lover.

As a child I rejected dolls in favor of tiny plastic horses to play with. While my friends played with their Barbie's, I yearned for the toy truck and horse trailer I saw at Woolworth's. I would spend hours with dad's scrap two-by-fours making corrals and pastures for my small plastic herd. At school I drew pictures of horses in my notebooks. From the library I checked out every book on horses they ever had. I read the whole Black Stallion series, all the CW Anderson books, all the Billy and Blaze books, all the Marguerite Henry books and more. I loved watching Robbie McDowell at the movies with My Friend Flicka and Thunderhead. My favorite TV show was Fury. Roy Rogers, the Cisco Kid, and Gene Autry only held my attention because of the horses they rode. It was my opinion that these silver screen cowboys would be nothing without the horses beneath them.

When I was only eight years old my playmate Sandy Cooper and I would plead with her mother to take us to a place that gave pony rides. These fat Shetlands had saddles with seat-belts to keep the children safe and balanced. After being strapped on, they would lead your pony to a ring with three fenced circles and turn it loose. The smallest ring was in the center. A pony that was turned into it would slowly walk around the circle and stop. The next circle was adjacent to it, and larger. The ponies that were led there would also walk around the ring but it took a few seconds longer. The furthest ring was the one I liked the best. It was used for the older children and when the pony was turned to travel around this ring, it trotted! Sandy and I would laugh as we bounced around the ring on our trotting ponies.

As I grew older I graduated to rental horses. It was a rare day for my own mother to drive my friend and I to a stable. More often than not, a friend that was as horse crazy as I would have a parent to take us. We lived for Saturdays when we could find a way to one of the stables where we could feed our passion. From there we could ride our gentle mounts over the grassy rolling hills of southern California or follow a canyon trail up into the foothills. I could think of nothing better to do in the whole world. By the time I was in high school I was familiar with the foundation bloodlines of my favorite breeds of horses. Quarter Horses, Appaloosas and Paints were on the top of my list. When the Los Angeles County Fair opened in the fall my girlfriend June and I spent hours at the horse barns looking at all the horses. The mixed aroma of shavings, Absorbine liniment and horse sweat was ambrosia to me.

After graduating high school I acquired a job and started saving towards the purchase of my first horse. I found a place to board a few miles from home and began my search. For the sum of one-hundred and seventy-five dollars I bought a pretty buckskin mare and named her Whiskey. She was well broke and a perfect first horse for me. Her manners were impeccable. If I wanted to walk she would walk. If I wanted to trot she would trot. To gallop, I just had to ask. Then she would calmly go back to a walk. She would go any direction I wanted without hesitation. Whiskey was like every other horse I had ever been around. Calm, well trained and obedient and I was under the impression all horses were just like her. I was in for a rude awakening.

My first horse, Whiskey.

My eighteenth birthday was a few months away when word came down from my parents that we were going to move. The good news was that we were headed towards Arizona and away from the congested city life that I loathed. The bad news was that we had no way to take my horse. I felt confident I could buy another horse in Arizona so I sold Whiskey to my friend and moved away.

We arrived in Chino Valley in midsummer and I immediately found another job. Mom and Dad had bought a place on the outskirts of town with a couple of acres suitable for dad's gardening and room enough to keep a horse. All I needed to do was find one. Oddly that turned out to be a difficult task. Although Chino Valley was a small rural town with lots of horses it seemed as though no one had any for sale. I watched the bulletin board at the local feed store and looked at the newspaper every day. I wasn't looking for anything in particular, just a horse, and in my limited experience any one of them would be just like Whiskey. They just came in different sizes and colors.

After several months of searching and even a trip to a livestock auction in Phoenix, I still had no horse. It was suggested to me that I try one of the local cattle ranchers to see if they had any stock available. The name Del Rio Ranch was put in my ear. It was there that I first saw the colt that would be my partner for the next thirty-two years.

Del Rio Ranch is located on old Highway 89 just a few miles north of Chino Valley. It has a rich history in the state from the time Arizona was a territory. When settlers started moving into the area word went out for them to watch for a small mountain that stuck up like a thumb. It was located near water. Lots of water. In fact, the area was sub-irrigated with an abundance of ground water seeping its way to the surface. This pre-historic volcanic cone that pointed upwards is located just to the east of the headwaters of the Verde River and the Del Rio Ranch. Other settlers sought out the larger landmark known as Thumb Butte near Prescott and settled there. As gold was discovered in the nearby creeks and mountains Prescott became a town of miners and ranchers. The farmers and home-steaders located where the water was, closer to the Verde River.

Back when Arizona was still a territory the Del Rio Ranch was designated as the first territorial capitol. Later on Fred Harvey used the ranch to provide his Harvey Houses with fresh beef, milk and produce. The railroad that ran through the ranch made the Harvey Houses and Grand Canyon readily accessible. In the late 1960's the ranch was owned by the Yarbro family.

Born in April of 1969 the bay colt spent most of his first three years at Del Rio Ranch in their Spring Canyon pasture. It was a remote place of rocky hillsides, cedar trees, pinyon pines, cliffs and wildlife. The chances of this herd of horses seeing a mountain lion was more likely than a human being.

For the most part the mares and foals were left to their own instincts. The foals grew up wary of predators and leery of people. They learned about rattlesnakes, coyotes, lions, deer and antelope. From their mothers the foals learned practical skills like pawing through the snow in winter to search for grass, where to cross the creeks and which hillsides to warm up on when the sun came out after a storm. For all intents and purposes the herd lived as close to being wild as their mustang neighbors to the north on the Navajo Reservation.

From the top of the highest hills the band of horses could see for miles and miles around. To the west was the spread out expanse of the Big Chino Valley reaching beyond Picacho Peak near Seligman all the way to the distant Tailholt Mountains. To the east the red rock cliffs of Sycamore Canyon stretched all the way to Sedona and Oak Creek. The south

Nothing missed Rocky's keen eyes.

fell away to the pine-studded Bradshaw Mountains and town of Prescott. This prehistoric lake bottom surrounded by mountain ranges was the panorama that lay beneath the tiny band of horses at the Del Rio Ranch.

Every fall the mares and foals were gathered up and brought into the ranch for weaning. The Yarbro youngsters all mounted up on their fastest horses for the event. Their father Bueford rode in his old pickup racing along with the half wild horses, sometimes flying airborne when his truck crossed a gully. When all arrived back at the holding pens the foals were separated from their mothers and left in a corral together. Over the next day or two each foal was caught by lariat and haltered for the first time. Most of the colts were gelded. Shots were given and lead ropes were left to drag from the halters when foals were released back into the corral. The foals were taught to lead and stand tied. This was not an easy process as these wild-eyed babies acted more like four hundred-pound jackrabbits than horses.

The foal crop that year included five foals. There was a buckskin, a grulla, two sorrels and a bay with a star in the middle of his forehead. Registration applications were filled out making note of color, markings, date of birth, and each was given a name. Bueford decided to name the bay colt Rocky after one of his sons. The colt's dam was Mix Fire. He blended the two names and the little bay was registered as Rocky Fire.

Rocky Yarbro riding Sut Breeze. Image courtesy of Rod Yarbro.

The colt was a reddish bay and very well built but a bit on the small-ish side. His sire was Sut Breeze, a grandson of Johnny Dial and Little Joe the Wrangler. Flying Bob and Joe Hancock being the next generation back. His dam Mix Fire was also a granddaughter of Johnny Dial and a horse called Hard Twist. Depth Charge, Cowboy, and Joe Reed were the next generation on her pedigree. Johnny Dial was a racing quarter horse that had been known to leave his jockeys in the gate due to his tremendous thrust at the start. All the ancestors in Rocky's bloodlines were outstanding foundation horses of the Quarter Horse breed. Bueford looked at the little bay colt and smiled. He sure had the bloodlines.

Rod Yarbro later related a story about the sire Sut Breeze as being the fastest horse he ever rode. He said the horse loved to chase a cow and once he started after one you'd better hang on. His brother Rocky was riding Sut Breeze one day when a cow ducked under and escaped into a hole in the thick prickly brush. Sut Breeze dived in after her and when they emerged on the far side his brother's nose and ears were shredded along with his new down jacket. A trail of feathers like a blizzard followed the obsessed horse and rider as they sped after their prey.

As fall turned into winter the weanlings continued with their halter lessons. Rocky Fire fought each step of the way. He hated the halter, hated the lead rope and wanted only to be free again roaming the canyons with his mother. He dreaded being caught and would run away to hide in the herd of weanlings at the far end of the corral when the wrangler approached. When caught by his lead rope Rocky Fire reared and fought against it. Eventually the obstinate colt was eased close enough to the side of the old red barn to tie him to a ring mounted on the wall. The rope was looped through the ring and tied securely, then the colt was left to figure things out on his own. The bay colt leaned back away from the wall, his head stretched out in front, feet braced. Then he'd jump forward and bounced off the wall, bracing himself against the barn again to fight from the other direction. Within a few minutes he tired and relaxed enough to put slack in the rope. The barn had won the battle this time, but the war was far from over.

Each day the weanlings were led to the side of the barn and tied. Some fought more than others did but eventually they all succumbed to the restriction of their freedom. During this time of confinement they were handled, scratched and brushed. Rocky Fire enjoyed the feeling of the brush along his neck. It reminded him of being scratched by his mother. So far it was the only part of his experience with man that he enjoyed. During one of his training sessions a low flying jet broke through the sound barrier and a loud sonic boom fell onto the ranch, rattling the windows in the barn and causing all the horses to scatter. Rocky, still tied to the wall, jumped backwards and pulled hard against the rope in panic. The ring weakened and broke loose along with a few feet of board. Rocky ran to the far end the corral, board dragging and slapping against his legs as he fled. He tried to hide in the herd but the dragging board caused all to panic and they fled in unison racing around the corral together. When the dust settled and the jittery colts slowed, the board was in splinters and the bay colt had a nasty cut below his left knee. The cut would heal but there would be a scar on his leg Rocky would carry the rest of his life.

During the winter months the weanlings were allowed access to a small pasture out behind the barns. By spring all of the weanlings had been sold except for the bay colt with the nasty wound. He was turned out that year to graze with the older ranch geldings. At the age of two he was still small for his age and was kept back again to give him time to grow. By the summer of his third year Rocky slicked off, healthy, healed and fat and was turned over to the horse wrangler to start under saddle.

The Christensens were relatives and lived just north of the Del Rio Ranch off Hwy 89. Their sons Raymond and Kennard were ranch raised and experienced at starting colts. All the young horses were started in the round pen. The pen had solid wood plank fencing that was almost ten feet tall. Inside the ground was covered in deep white sand. It was here that Rocky learned to accept the saddle and rider. The boys took their time and soon Rocky was their star pupil. He learned to turn left and right, stop and go and how to back up. When taken out to work around the cattle they discovered Rocky had a real knack for it. The little bay horse enjoyed pushing the cows around. He was a natural. It shouldn't have come as much of a surprise as his bloodlines were full of hard working cow horses. So impressed and confident were the boys that once when a calf made a break, his rider shook out a loop and urged Rocky after it. The calf was roped.

What happened next was a chain reaction that undid all the trust and training Rocky had acquired. The calf reversed direction and went behind Rocky faster than he could turn. The saddle slipped, the rider bailed, and the rope went under the horse, calf still attached. Rocky Fire panicked and blew like Krakatoa. As if modeling for a Charlie Russell painting, the bay colt, calf, rider and rope all tangled up together in a terrible wreck. It was a miracle that no one was seriously injured. However the damage to Rocky Fire was deep and would on occasion bubble up to the top throughout his life.

The year was 1972. It was mid September and I had just turned eighteen. The Vietnam War was starting to wind down and the troubles of the world seemed far away to me as I drove up the gravel driveway to the Del Rio ranch. The first glimpse I had of Rocky was of him heading back out to pasture with a handful of other young horses. I liked the looks of a dark grulla filly that was also there, but my eye went back to the pretty bay with the star. They had just been turned out for the day. The late summer sun bounced of his cinnamon colored coat. His shiny black legs matched his mane and tail. The only white on him was a large spot in the middle of his forehead and a faint snip between his nostrils.

The Yarbro's showed me the registration papers on the bay three-year-old gelding. I knew his bloodlines from all the research I had done and was impressed with his famous relatives. An appointment was made the next day for me to ride him in the round pen. I was excited about the possibility of being able to own such a nice young horse with so many Champions on his papers.

The next afternoon I arrived at the ranch. Rocky was already in the round pen and was being ridden by a young Mexican man. He dismounted when he saw me and I walked forward to mount the pretty bay. Rocky took a couple steps as I found my seat. It felt good to be back on a horse. I hadn't ridden since I had sold Whiskey. Rocky stepped out and began walking around the perimeter of the small wooden round pen. He sunk deep in the sand as he walked. After going around several times I clucked and pushed him into a trot, slowed again and turned him into the center of the pen. He did not understand neck reining. The Mexican told me he had been ridden 'ten saddles'. I rode him around the pen for several more minutes at a walk and trot, then dismounted. He was perfect. I patted him on the neck, then handed the reins back over to the Mexican and walked up to the Yarbro home.

Mr. Yarbro wanted five hundred dollars for the colt. I thought that was kind of high considering the horse market averaged closer to two hundred for a well broke horse, and under a hundred for anything someone could ride through an auction ring. I had sold Whiskey for a hundred and seventy-five. My entire savings were four hundred, so I offered that as a down payment and promised to bring the balance as soon as I received my next paycheck.

A few days later I returned with the last of the money and Rocky was brought down from the corrals for me. I did not even own a saddle at

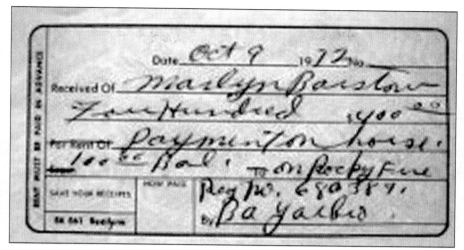

Down payment receipt for Rocky Fire.

this point. I had to borrow one to ride my new horse the eight miles back home. The Mexican holding Rocky mounted another horse and rode with me the half mile to the ranch gate.

The next mile was through a sub-irrigated pasture. Riding alone I directed my new horse around the really soggy areas and between the few cows that lived there. I dismounted to open the gate at the other end and walked Rocky through. He took interest in his surroundings but never offered to jump or spook at anything. His ears always pointed straight ahead except when I touched him with hand or heel. Then the ear on the side that was touched would flick back and then return to its locked and forward position. From the pasture I rode him out Road Four North to Highway 89. The easement along the highway was very wide and we followed it for several miles. At Center Street I could head east again and take Road One East to Road Two South where I lived. The ride was uneventful and I arrived home safely and very pleased with my beautiful registered American Quarter Horse gelding. After unsaddling I put Rocky in his large corral and threw him some hay. He went out into the center of the pen and rolled, then took interest in any neighboring horses he could see.

A few weeks after Rocky's arrival a neighbor brought home a donkey. He put it in an adjoining yard and upon seeing Rocky, it brayed loudly, and trotted over to say hello with its long ears a flapping. The sight was terrifying to the young horse that had never seen such a deformed animal. It was Rocky's undoing and his flight instinct drove him across his pen and right through the wire fence at high speed. I grabbed a halter and ran next door to retrieve him. Blood trickled down his left front leg from a couple of surface cuts. I doctored him up and put him back into his pen. This time he just looked at the long-eared critter suspiciously as he ate his hay. The fence was more smashed than broken and straightened out almost good as new.

I gave him a few days off from riding and then the weather turned nasty. It was October in the mile high country. Finally the sun came out and I had time to ride my beautiful horse. I had purchased an old roping saddle and a bridle with a nice Tom Thumb bit and was good to go. I led Rocky out and tied him to the four by four wooden corner post that held up the carport. As I brushed Rocky's coat I noticed how thick his winter coat had become. I placed the saddle blankets on him and threw the saddle up onto his back. His head went up and he snorted but I paid no mind. I reached under and grabbed the cinch. In the process of tightening it Rocky pulled back hard and quick against the post stretching taut the rope he was tied with. And then as quickly as he went back he jumped forward and slammed his face against the corner of the four by four.

I had managed to jump back from the thousand pounds of frantic horse in front of me. He pulled back again, but with less force this time, then came to a stiff-legged stop. The lead rope knot was tight but I was able to untie him from the post before he went on a rampage again. I was afraid he'd yank down the carport roof if he pulled back one more time. Turning him towards me I could see the blood seeping from the foot long crease down the length of his face. As he took his first step he broke into a bucking fit and jumped around me in a circle. I yelled and pulled on the lead and he finally stopped but I could see he was not a happy horse. I wasn't sure if I should ride him at this point. My concern was that he'd knocked himself silly against that post. I finally led him out into a small field and rode him around the perimeter quietly a couple of times then put him up.

After the incident with the carport my dad built a tie rack for me. It consisted of two cedar posts buried in the ground with a pole nailed between them. Just like the ones you see in the old westerns. What it should have been was two six-inch diameter iron pipes sunk and cemented about three feet into the ground with a welded four-inch wide iron bar between them. More like something secure enough to hold an elephant. Dad's new tie rack worked fine. Just so long as I didn't tie Rocky to it. The birds liked it for a perch and it added that 'western' ranch look to the place. My horse sense was still not working correctly and I made the mistake of using it for its intended purpose. I tied Rocky to it so I could brush him down.

You'll never guess what happened next. For no apparent reason Rocky set back and pulled against the rail. The two posts only swayed a little bit but the six-foot long rail snapped loose from the nails and left with Rocky. He ran around the property twice before stopping. I walked carefully up to him and gingerly unhooked the lead rope with pole still attached to leave it where it lay.

A couple of days later a neighbor rode over on her horse and after lunging Rocky to get the kinks out we rode off together towards Prescott. We rode along side Highway 89 until we passed the entrance to the Deep Well Ranch near the Prescott airport. Rocky was suspicious of the Deep Well Ranch's mailbox standing alone near the highway and gave it a wide berth. On our ride back to Chino my companion's well broke and aged horse however won the 'spooking horse' prize. She nearly lost control of him as he freaked out and refused to pass the two brightly-painted twenty-foot tall wood Kachinas at the entrance to a trailer park. Rocky paid them no mind at all and couldn't figure out what his companion was so upset about.

Rocky Fire and myself, 1972.

In November my friend June from my high school days came to visit. The weather had been cold and I hadn't ridden Rocky in a week. I got him out and started to exercise him on the lunge line. When I saddled him up I asked June if she would ride him while I lunged him, thinking this would be a safe way to let her ride my new horse. June and I had enjoyed many hours of riding together when I lived in California and we both loved horses. June climbed up in the saddle and she moved Rocky off at a walk. About half way around the second circle I clucked to him to trot. His head went down and he flew into a bucking fit. June was thrown before Rocky had completed the circle. I was shocked and she was stunned. Rocky had quit bucking but was watching us from the end of the lead, head up and snorting. I felt horrible! I had no idea he would come apart and buck off my best friend. Thank goodness she wasn't hurt. Although I kept Rocky for the next thirty-two years June never wanted to get on him again.

On Christmas Day that winter I had the day off, and even though it was brisk there was no snow and the sun was shining. It was a good day to go riding and Rocky hadn't been out for awhile. My nephew David was visiting and I invited him to come out and watch me ride my horse. As it turned out it would be more fun for him than the Super Bowl. That was the day Rocky made a believer out of me.

After saddling Rocky up I led him back into his large corral with the thought of keeping my nephew safe in the event there was an event. I stopped Rocky in the center of the corral and placed my foot in the stirrup. After sitting down in the saddle and finding the other stirrup Rocky went straight up into the air and came down hard. From my vantage point his head and neck were missing. In fact the only thing between the horizon and myself was the saddle horn. The sensation of being lifted so high by that invisible force beneath me was unnerving. I was just along for the ride, which was now circling the corral. As I looked down to my right I could see the tops of the green T-posts way below. A thought flashed through my mind that Rocky was capable of bucking right over the top of the fence without even touching it. His leaps were growing more violent. I could hear him grunting each time he hit the dirt.

My book learning came to mind and I remembered someone said to pull the horses' head up and to the side to get him under control. I reached down grabbing the rein by my right and with all my strength pulled Rocky's head up. At that point his thousand pounds of thrust overcame my one hundred thirty pounds of pressure. He straightened his neck back out, taking the rein and me along with it. I went over his right shoulder and hit the ground hard. For a moment I was stunned. Rocky quit bucking after circling the corral another time.

I stood up and saw my nephew standing speechless on the far side of the fence. All I could think of was another line from a book. "If you get thrown, you need to get right back on." So that's what I did. I caught Rocky and climbed back on. As soon as I got my seat the rodeo was on. It felt like an eternity but I rode that bronc till he stood. Then I carefully stepped off. I was a wreck. Shaking from the adrenaline, I led Rocky back to the barn and unsaddled him. I think my nephew had run to the house to sell tickets but the party was over. As I limped back to the house I started to feel the damage. There were no broken bones from my fall but I was a mess. The next morning I was expected back at work and I arrived there bent over and black and blue.

I was a cashier at the old Yellow Front store in Prescott. It was all I could do to stand at the register, bent over, checking people out. One of my co-workers brought me a tall stool to sit on. Another said I should visit her chiropractor. So during my lunch break that's exactly what I did. The good doctor took me right in. Say what you want about them, but all I know is that I walked in folded over and came out standing tall. If he could have only adjusted my mind also. Physically my body was healing, but I had acquired a new emotion when it came to horses....fear.

A few days after my rodeo debut I met an old rancher from the Cornville area. He and his wife were now living at the Arizona Pioneers Home just a few blocks from where I worked. I had seen him in the store several times but today as he checked out he noticed my scrapes and bruises and asked me what the 'other' guy looked like. I then told him I owned a horse named Rocky the Fire breathing dragon and that it was this horse that had done the damage. We talked for several minutes until the next person showed up at my register to check out. The rancher stepped away and waited for the customer to leave. He then asked me if I would like him to come look at the horse and help if possible. My first thoughts were to decline and contact Harry Vold to see if he wanted the horse for his bucking string. Instead I set up a time and gave the old cowboy directions to my home.

It was just after noon several days later that a faded pale green Datsun pickup came down our driveway. On the front of the vehicle a brass saddle horn was bolted onto the hood in lieu of a hood ornament. Mom and Dad came out to meet the man that had offered to help their daughter with her unruly horse. The truck stopped in the gravel driveway and they watched the tall cowboy emerged from his tiny truck. He introduced himself as Dale Girdner, a longtime Arizona resident from the Verde Valley area. He was over six feet tall in his dusty cowboy boots. On his head he wore a shapeless weathered cowboy hat. A pearl-buttoned well worn western shirt and faded jeans finished his attire. His face was thin and bore evidence of a lifetime of working in the great outdoors. His eyes were blue as the sky above him and his smile as warm as the Arizona sun. Born in 1899, Dale came out west from Kansas with his parents as a small boy. He spoke about the history of Arizona, cattle, and his ranch he'd owned near the banks of Oak Creek near the town of Sedona.

As Dale continued speaking with my parents I walked out to the corral and returned with my horse. Rocky stood calmly while my parents and Dale finished their conversation. After my parents went back to the house Dale and I turned our attentions back to the unpretentious horse standing at the end of my lead rope. I explained without embellishment the events that had occurred leading up to and including my Christmas Day disaster. All I wanted at this point was to make the horse stop bucking. I suggested perhaps that we could hobble him. I didn't know what else to do.

Dale asked me to go about saddling the horse just like I always did so that he could see me interact with Rocky and perhaps find out where the problem lay. Rocky stood cemented to the ground as I quickly brushed him off and put the saddle blankets on. Before I saddled him I brought out a pair of leather hobbles and put them on his front legs. Before placing the saddle on his back I got out a lariat and looped it between the hobbles, then gave the other end to Dale. I asked Dale to jerk him off his feet if he started bucking. What I didn't know was that Dale was not convinced this motionless little horse standing so quietly next to him was the terror I made him out to be.

I picked up my saddle and slowly set it down on Rocky's back. I was careful not to let stirrups or cinches slap down against him. I walked to the far side and adjusted stirrups and straps then came back around to pull up the cinch. I did so slowly and with much trepidation.

The saddle was secure. Rocky had not moved a muscle. He had just stiffened them. All of them. To my shock and horror Dale reached out for the saddle horn and shook it forward and back slightly to settle the saddle. Before he finished the lead rope ripped through my hand as Rocky left the earth. I heard the whiz as the lariat burned Dale's hand as he tried to regain a grip, but it was too late.

The Counterfeit!

Rocky was airborne, bucking, bellowing and farting for all he was worth across the field. If the hobbles slowed him down any you couldn't see it. My plan had failed. Dale looked at me sheepishly and said, "I didn't believe you. He's a counterfeit." Then he inspected the rope burns across his palms. After Rocky came to a stop across the far end of the field Dale asked, "Could you have rode him?" I gave him my honest answer. "No." At this point I didn't even want to think about getting on him.

While Rocky was still stopped at the far end of the field I walked over and picked up his lead rope. He was still snorty but stood still long enough for Dale to remove the hobbles. As I led him back to where we started Dale spoke again and told me "We forgot to do one very important thing." "What's that?" I asked. Dale just spoke one word "Pray." Dale then went on. "I'm a Christian, and we forgot to pray. We need help from a higher power, the feller that created this little horse." A moment later he added, "Little Sis, your horse is an outlaw. Horses learn habits. They don't understand the difference between good habits and bad habits. They just learn habits and this one is going to be tough to break. But I'm willing to help if you want me to." I agreed. I hadn't given up all hope yet. Perhaps this kindly old rancher could help and make up for my lack of knowledge and skill.

Dale came out again the next day and began his Boot Camp for Obstinate Horses. At the same time I was drafted into Common Sense Cowboy Horsemanship 101 and I didn't even know it. Dale dripped with knowledge of horses and I was a sponge. His seventy plus years as a cattle rancher, horseman, and Christian opened up a whole new world to me. Within a week Dale had taken Rocky over to the Long Meadow Ranch in Williamson Valley. Dale was doing day work there and knew putting Rocky's mind on cattle would help him. Dale told me that as a young man he had rode his share of bucking horses. He used to rope wild mustangs in the Verde Valley and break them the old 'cowboy' way. Choke them down, throw a saddle on, climb up and ride them till they quit bucking. Then repeat it again the next day until the horse decided it was just too much effort. Over the years he found a better way that was easier on both man and horse. Dale was a horse whisperer long before the term was invented.

Mentally, Rocky was a mess. To begin his re-education, Dale put him in the round pen and started working his rope around him. He'd throw a loop towards the horse and Rocky would stampede around the perimeter of the pen. Before an hour was up Dale could throw it over Rocky's head and catch him, then release him again. The rope was everywhere. Over, under and in between. It went across Rocky's back and under his belly and between his legs. As the rope danced around the pen Dale kept up a one-sided conversation with the wide-eyed colt. Dale told me that someday this horse might get his leg caught in something and he had better learn not to panic. There was no better time to learn that than now, so within a few minutes Rocky's hind leg was sidelined and he was fighting the restraint by himself around the corral.

When he came to a three-legged stop, Dale went up to Rocky and asked him how he had gotten himself in such a predicament. He released the leg and played up the role of being the savior of entangled horses.

Over the next few days Rocky practiced standing on three legs a lot. Horse hobbles are used to slow a horse down. A sideline will pretty much

Dale Girdner working with an unbroke colt. Image by Claudette Simpson, courtesy of Sharlott Hall Museum.

bring one to a stop. A long thick cotton rope is looped around the horse's neck at the widest point near the shoulder, then tied with a bowline knot so it will not tighten. The other end is looped around the heel of a hind foot and raised off the ground a foot or so by re-threading it through the loop around the neck and then tied in that position. The horse therefore is tied to itself and half their engine is disabled. Kind of like a vehicle running on four cylinders instead of eight. Barely moving.

Dale reassured Rocky all through this process by stroking his neck and talking quietly to him. It became as natural for Rocky to stand on three legs as it was for another horse to be tied to a hitching rail. Dale was always the one that came to Rocky's rescue and released him. Trust was beginning to bloom, if ever so slightly. The next step was to bring the saddle back into the picture. However by this time Rocky had learned to do some arithmetic. Put three down and carry one. Of his legs, that is.

Dale had sidelined Rocky and the horse stood stiffly as the saddle was placed upon his back. He quivered as the cinch was tightened. With everything secured Dale stepped away and left Rocky alone to his figure things out. Before Dale reached the edge of the corral Rocky exploded and did the best he could to buck around the corral. Half way around Rocky lost his balance and tumbled down onto the deep sand. Unable to get up with his fourth leg restrained, he finally lay back down on the sand and blew angry breaths into the air.

Dale waited a few minutes as Rocky gave up on his struggles. Then he calmly walked over to the horse and looked down at him. Reaching down to stroke his neck, Dale asked "Now what have you gone and done to get yourself into a predicament this time?" Rocky lay his head back after a tiny attempt to get up and groaned. Dale walked around the horse stroking him here and there. Then backed up to the horse's rump and using it as a seat, sat down. Dale looked at the prone animal and said "Rocky, you done wore me out. I hope you don't mind if I set here a spell to rest a bit."

Dale called me into the pen and had me sit next to him on Rocky's rump. A few minutes later we got up, and Dale rescued Rocky. When Rocky regained his feet, all four of them, Dale calmly led the horse around the pen. Rocky, humbled, showed no desire to start bucking. He unsaddled Rocky and repeated the process. This time when Dale finished securing the saddle and walked away, Rocky stood. The next day the process was repeated, but this time Dale walked me through it and I did it by myself several times and though Rocky was still a little snorty, he knew bucking would be futile.

Dale and I left Rocky alone to think about things while we saddled up a pair of the Long Meadow's ranch horses. We were going to ride several miles south to the calving pasture to check on the cows and Rocky was going to tag along. Dale ponied Rocky with his lariat tied to the halter, sometimes keeping next to him, and other times he'd let Rocky out to nearly the end of the thirty-foot rope driving him ahead. The pasture was dotted with scrub oak and Dale used these natural barriers to direct Rocky to the left or right as we went along. We rode down sandy washes and across rocky gullies, up mountain sides and across small meadows.

After a couple of hours Dale told me "Little Sis, I think it's time you rode your horse."

My mouth went dry. I put the horse I was riding into a small holding pen to wait for our return. Dale checked Rocky's cinch and swapped the bridle from the horse I had been riding to Rocky. Dale remounted his horse and still leading Rocky with the lariat, dallied him up close. I was shaking. Before I climbed aboard Dale said a prayer to keep me safe and the horse calm. Prayer had become a common occurrence as he worked with Rocky. I knew I needed it now. For courage if nothing else. Rocky stood as I climbed up. I blew out a long breath and found my seat. Dale led Rocky off and I expected the worst. It was the first time Rocky had been ridden since Christmas. Rocky wasn't the only one with trust issues.

After five minutes or so I felt better and Dale gave us a little more rope. In a half-hour he turned us loose. I was riding my horse again. I wish I could say how excited and confident I was but I couldn't. I did not trust this horse under me.

As we rode along towards the heifer pasture the beautiful scenery helped distract me from my fear. We made our way along a game trail wedged between granite boulders larger than the horses. Scattered pinyon pines and cedar trees grew alongside the prickly pear and staghorn cactus. The February sky was cold and clear. Quail were whistling their warnings as we trespassed through their territory. As we topped a small hill a Hereford cow came into view. Standing next to her was a newborn calf. Just past her a few yards away stood a large coyote. Our presence sent the coyote back into the brush. We watched him as he disappeared back down the far side of the hill, snaking in and out of the brush for cover.

Rocky quickly turned his head to the right towards an adjacent hill a thousand yards away. It took a moment for me to focus on what had caught his attention. A small group of mule deer were trotting along the side of the hill away from us. More deer joined them. Dale and I sat on our horses and the four of us watched as we counted over forty muleys come out of the oak brush and disappear around the side of the hill.

The experience awakened me to the wilder side of Arizona. Many vast areas of the state were still as raw and untouched as the day it was created. I loved the feeling of being miles from anywhere, isolated, remote, with no signs or sounds of civilization to be seen or heard. The only sounds I could hear was the wind blowing through the pinyon pines, the breathing of my horse, and the creak of my saddle when I moved. This was heaven on earth. This was the feeling of complete freedom! I wanted to be able to enjoy this moment again and again and I now understood how to make it happen. It would be on the back of a horse. My horse! I was determined to do whatever it took to make the horse beneath me my companion and link to this infinite Arizona wilderness.

Dale kept Rocky at the Long Meadow Ranch for several weeks. When spring roundup began at the Indian Rock Ranch near Yava, Dale took Rocky there and I joined them for several days of gathering cows. My experience with cattle up to this point had only been the black and white spotted variety that walked into a dairy barn twice a day. These range mamas were a different critter. Rocky and I rode at the back of the herd keeping the stragglers caught up with the main body. Rocky loved walking behind the cows. He quickly picked up the job of watching for the one that slowed or veered away so he could get her back in the group. I hardly had to touch him with my heel or rein to turn him towards a cow. The shift in my weight was enough of a cue for him to move out. I had begun to enjoy riding my horse again.

Dale had taught us both new habits to replace the old ones. He also ingrained into me a whole collection of new habits that I didn't even know I was lacking. The first of which was the proper way to bridle a horse. Dale was used to handling uncooperative horses, colts and wild mustangs. His method worked for all and I repeated the procedure just as he taught me ever since.

"Little Sis," Dale told me, "First you have to catch your horse." Dale picked up an empty burlap feed sack and laid it on the ground. Then he folded it in half lengthwise. He took out his pocket knife and began cutting halfway down the length of the bag a few inches from the seam through all four layers and followed it all the way back up to the open end. "You may not have a bucket of feed available every time to catch your horse. You can throw some corn in this burlap nose bag and tie it on your saddle."

He picked up the bag and turned it inside out so the raw edges and threads were on the outside. Then he tied the long strips he had cut together. That was the part to go over the horse's head and hold the bag up to his face so he could eat and not lose any feed. The flaps that now hung down on the front and back of the bag would also be knotted together so the horse couldn't step on them and it made the bag a tighter fit against the horse's face.

This was the original cowboy nosebag. The horses all loved them. Each could have their own and if another horse tried to steal their feed they could just pick up their head and walk away with it. Unlike a bucket it was comfortable against their face, there was no clanking of metal and very little feed fell on the ground. One of the side benefits was that once a horse had this on its face it could be used like a halter just enough for the horse to think he's caught. If and when a bag broke or finally wore out a trip to the feed room with a pocketknife produced another in just a few minutes.

It was easy to catch a horse this way. Dale said he could walk out to his herd of horses and hold up the bags and they'd come a running even if they were a half section away. "The way to a horse's halter is through their stomach" Dale stated.

Then Dale showed me how to put my long split reins in a circle around my horse's neck before I removed the nosebag. When the bag came off the bridle went on. I moved my right hand, reins still circling the neck to the top of Rocky's head and rested my hand between his ears. This left my left hand free to guide the bridle over his nose and my thumb free to slip into the corner of his mouth. It became another habit that Rocky and I learned together.

The first day I had off after roundup I met Dale back at the Indian Rock Ranch. Dale and I were both pleased with Rocky's rehabilitation and Dale thought Rocky was ready to go back home. But instead of giving Rocky a trailer ride Dale suggested I should just ride him home. It was only thirty-five miles or so across country and he was confident the little horse would do fine. Dale would drive ahead and catch us about halfway near Skull Valley. I thought it was a great idea so I saddled Rocky early that morning and we left the ranch at a trot. I wasn't concerned about getting lost as there were so many natural landmarks I could use to keep my bearing. I wasn't about to miss this opportunity to fade back into the raw wilderness at the far reaches of the Indian Rock Ranch. It would be the longest ride I had ever taken on Rocky and it would help the bond between us to grow. I think this was part of Dale's unspoken plan all along.

At the end of the mile long ranch dirt driveway we slowed to cross the blacktop highway and then went through the gate that accessed the flat mesas to the west. The plan was to ride to the top of the mesa and follow the jeep trail until it turned south. Then we'd turn towards the north and aim towards Skull Valley skirting Martin Mountain on the western slope. I was completely unfamiliar with the area and was told by the ranch foreman that I should follow the fence line in order to locate the gate.

Rocky had a long swinging trot that really covered the ground. We made it to the bottom of the mesa in a half-hour. He loved being out in the middle of nowhere as much as I did. We slowed to climb the mesa and reaching the top turned to look back across the miles of high desert we had just traveled. At the far end we could see the cottonwoods growing along Kirkland Creek. In their shade I could barely see the tops of the ranch buildings that we had departed from earlier that morning.

Turning Rocky back to the task at hand we rode away from the mesa's edge and followed the dusty jeep trail. The sun was warm on my back and it hadn't occurred to me yet that in my haste to depart I had done so without a canteen. There would probably be water holes ahead for the cattle and springs in the canyons. Dale had taught me how to read a cow trail and which way would lead to water. The morning was still young and I wasn't concerned. I should be able to meet up with Dale before noon. Rocky could drink where the cattle did and I could suffice with a windmill or spring. Provided there was one.

Before too long the jeep trail swung off to the south and I began looking across the flat mesa in all directions for the fence I was told to follow. When my eyes failed to find anything resembling a fence I reined Rocky towards Skull Valley and decided we'd find it eventually. The western edge of the mesa sloped off gently and towards the bottom we found a large stock pond holding the remnants of the last spring rain. Rocky drank his fill but the water was too dirty for my taste. Cattle had been using this tank on a regular basis. Their muddy tracks surrounded its shallow edges.

Rocky and I traveled on. There were no cow or game trails for us to follow. The bay horse and I were the only objects moving out across the high lonesome. The last evidence of man was a few faint hoof prints from a shod horse that appeared and disappeared into the tall gama grass. Many miles away to the north I could see the Ferguson Valley with its Peavine Railroad curling its way towards the horizon. Martin Mountain was now at our right. Rocky and I had come a long way. At the base of that mountain would be Skull Valley and Dale. We were heading in the right direction.

The scenery around us was unending. To the west I could make out Sheridan Mountain and Sycamore Creek. Soon Granite Mountain came into view. Had I just had a canteen of water with me things would have been too perfect for words. I was starting to get a little dry. The terrain around us had changed from malapai rock to granite. Far below us I could see the bladed strip of dirt road that would lead us to Skull Valley. Between us and that road was an entire forest of granite boulders, some thirty feet tall or more. It seemed like God had taken his last load of leftover boulders and dumped them right here. It would be a labyrinth to ride through. As we walked down into the maze I spied a fence line coming in from the east. At last, the long lost fence. Or perhaps it may have been a different one altogether. Either way, I made a decision to work our way towards it and hoped to find some clean water trapped between the rocks.

Following rabbit trails we slowly squeezed our way past one formation then another. After about forty-five minutes of stop, go, back up and retrace our steps, we came to the fence. A few yards this side of it a trickle of water ran for a short distance before disappearing beneath another boulder. Dismounting I got down on my hands and knees and bent down to the clear water and sipped slowly. It was warm but wet and I spent several minutes drinking and then wetting my face to cool off.

Refreshed I was ready to tackle the barbed wire barrier and continue on our journey. If only I had brought a pair of pliers with me! Or better yet a fence tool. Standing on a rock I could see up and down the fence line quite a ways. No gate as far as I could see. How anyone managed to plant cedar posts in this overgrown rock garden was beyond my comprehension. Yet here it was and I had to get Rocky through it. Following the fence downhill I came across a small four-foot section that crossed over a granite boulder. If I could just loosen and push down the top two wires perhaps I could get Rocky up on the rock to step over to the other side. The fence was stretched tighter than a E string on a two dollar fiddle. It took a half-hour for me to loosen the wire with my bare fingers from the post enough for it to drop. The top wire was still a foot in the air stretched tight over the rock. I couldn't get it to drop any lower.

I was certain I could get Rocky to follow me up onto the rock. But if he tripped on the wire or slid on the rocks slick surface he would certainly slip a leg between the rock and the wire. The result would be lots of cuts and perhaps a horse trapped between a rock and a sharp place. If that happened I wouldn't be able to help him or get help from anyone. We were in a very remote isolated spot. A bad feeling came over me and I knew this was a really stupid thing to attempt.

Walking back over to the trickle of water I took another pause to refresh then mounted Rocky and backtracked up our trail. This was frustrating to say the least. I could see where I needed to be yet I couldn't find a way to get there. From the angle of the sun I could tell my daylight would be an issue soon. I had to make a decision. I could spend the remaining hours of daylight trying to find a way through the rock maze and fence. If I failed, I would be stuck out here overnight and I knew how my parents and Dale would worry. This was also mountain lion and bear country and I had no weapon. Add to that the fact I had no water and my decision was made. I had to get back to the Indian Rock while there was still daylight to do so.

Rocky had packed me over fifteen miles or so of rough rocky country thus far. Still every step he took his ears remained pointed forward and he was alert. We had a long hot late afternoon ride back to the ranch. Stopping to let Rocky drink again at the cow tank I began feeling the effects of dehydration. Being the font of wisdom as most eighteen-year-old's are, I continued to make poor decisions and decided to add another one to this day's adventure. I dismounted and drank along with Rocky. Not much. Just enough for one swallow and wet my tongue. It was a long ways back to the ranch from here.

Rocky seemed happy to be heading back. I trotted him along hoping the trail would end before the daylight did. We reached the side of the mesa and started down the rough trail just as the sun dipped behind the mountain. At the bottom I chose to head south to the ranch headquarters where I knew there was a phone. Rocky was starting to slow his walk. A mile away from the barn Rocky's ears started bobbing back and forth as he walked. It was the only time I saw his ears flop in the thirty-two years we had together. He was one tired horse. The next day I learned about dysentery and Rocky got a ride home.

After a doctor prescribed remedy of Lomotil I quickly recovered and was anxious to start riding again. Rocky still had a lot of rough edges to sand down. He didn't know how to neck rein very well, I still sidelined him for saddling, and I dare not tie him to anything yet. "One step at a time" Dale said.

The first few rides away from home Dale rode him. Our first destination was Table Mountain about six miles or so to the west. We chose to climb the north side of the furthest peak. The old gelding that I had borrowed from the neighbors slipped and sometimes stumbled as he climbed over the larger malapai rocks near the rim. As I watched Rocky go before me I was amazed at how he climbed through the pile of rocks like a deer. He never slowed down and was sure of his footing. From the top of the mountain we could see the snow capped San Francisco Peaks over eighty miles away. Behind us was Williamson Valley and to the east was the town of Chino. It was another beautiful panorama of Arizona I has grown to love so much. Over the next few years I would ride Rocky to the top of this mountain many, many times just to marvel at the view.

We rode across this grassy top of the flat mesa and discovered a wall of stacked rocks. It led to a series of smaller rock walls that connected to each other, each about ten feet square. Having never seen an Indian ruin before, I asked Dale about it. He said he wasn't sure if it was or not. It might just have been a fortress for defending themselves or a hide for hunting game. After looking it over for awhile we headed back down the mountain. At the bottom Dale shook out a loop and let Rocky get used to dragging the rope behind him. Then as we covered the miles towards home, Dale started roping rabbit brush and dragging it.

For the most part Rocky didn't care, but when Dale roped a dead tree limb that was lying on the ground Rocky took notice. Dale turned Rocky towards it and stopped him. The limb was twenty feet away. Dale gave it a tug and it rolled towards him. Rocky bowed his neck and snorted. Dale moved Rocky a few feet closer. He pulled it again. Rocky cocked his head and looked the dead limb over carefully. Dale gave it a series of little jerks until Rocky got bored with it. Then he rode Rocky up close so he could get a smell of the animated tree limb. Rocky touched it with his nose and then stood there as if asking "Don't we have someplace to go? This is a waste of my time!" Dale agreed and turned Rocky away, dragging the limb at the end of his rope. Rocky cocked his head towards it a few times but then gave it little attention. Slowly Dale shortened his rope as we rode along and before we had covered the next mile Rocky was calmly dragging that limb a few feet behind him like it belonged there.

On another day we rode out east of Chino onto the Deep Well Ranch that lay to the south. There were areas along the foothills that were spotted with staghorn cactus growing as tall as our stirrups. Dale used these as a reining training aide. He rode Rocky back and forth around and through the cactus. Like Helen Keller making the connection between the running water and her teachers hand motions, Rocky started making the connection between the feel of rein on his neck, the shift of Dales weight, and the direction he should chose to go around the cactus. If Rocky started to go the wrong direction, Dale stopped him and the backed him up to go the right way. Before long it became a dance. The cowboy and horse swayed together between the cactus first left, then right, then left, like partners in a slow moving waltz.

A few weeks later Dale began working with another young horse named Carmelita who was boarded just around the corner from our place We decided that on my next day off to ride to the Verde River together. We left about eight o'clock in the morning and headed east onto the Deep Well Ranch a mile or so away. From there Dale led me to the gates that crossed the railroad tracks and on to the Perkins Ranch. Both young horses behaved well. The younger filly was comfortable with Rocky as a companion and Rocky was just glad to be going somewhere.

As we rode along Dale sang old cowboy songs. Sometimes I knew them, like Little Joe the Wrangler and I would sing along. Others came from the real old time cowboys in the late 1800's and I had never heard them. These were the songs that Dale grew up with. He taught several to me on our rides together.

Crossing the railroad tracks to the east we could ride out further onto the grasslands and then head north. There was a sandy wash that split the prairie between Chino and Mingus Mountain known as Granite Creek. We used it as a guide that would point us towards the river. Following it north we eventually found the road that trailed the El Paso Natural Gas pipeline, then used it as our path all the way to the Verde. The grasslands turned to low hills that skirted the north end of Lonesome Valley. The trail became rocky and we could smell the Verde River before we could see it. The scent of wet earth and damp sycamore leaves sifted up from the canyons below. Between clumps of cattail and salt cedar we could see the occasional sparkle of water winding its way along the canyon floor.

Hereford cattle grazed the short grass along the edges of the banks, lifting their heads as we rode into view. The river itself was just a few yards wide and shallow with only occasional pockets of deeper water for the huge dark carp that lived there to hide in.

The canyon that hid it had white and reddish layered walls of rock that stretched upwards to the turquoise Arizona sky. We let our horses

Rocky cooling off in the Verde River.

walk out into the cool clear water. They drank their fill as Dale and I admired our surroundings.

The water level barely came up to the horse's knees. Carmelita started to paw at the water and Dale encouraged her across to the other bank. She had wanted to lay down and roll in the water. Rocky used his nose to splash the water back and forth playfully for a minute, then I followed Dale to the other side. As we jumped up the far bank I noticed the tree to our left was chiseled in an hourglass shape a foot or so from its base. I pointed it out to Dale who had already noticed it. Yes, he said, there were beavers on the Upper Verde.

This canyon would be my favorite destination to ride to over the next few years. Rocky brought me here many, many times. More often than not, I rode alone with Rocky across the fourteen miles of prairie and foothills that stretched between my home and the Verde. Seldom would I have company. Leaving early in the morning and setting out at a trot, Rocky and I would arrive at the river by 11a.m. and then return home before dark. It was a beautiful place to ride and I never tired of it. I loved the desolation of the prairie, the beauty of the foothills and the refreshing coolness of the water.

Because Rocky sometimes humped up in the mornings when I first saddled him I still went through the procedure of tying up his hind leg. It had only been a couple of months since we had started retraining him and Dale said it was best to err on the side of caution. Continue the same procedure, the same routine, make it a habit. After tightening the cinch I'd spend a minute or two checking straps and breast collar, load my saddle bags with a bite to eat and water, then let Rocky's leg down.

Dale made it clear with no uncertain terms that I should always lead Rocky out a few steps to make sure he wasn't going to blow up into a bucking fit. As I led Rocky those first few steps his front legs would stiffen and he'd shudder as he walked like a powder keg under extreme pressure. After walking forward a few yards he'd relax and I'd stop him, check the cinch and climb up into the saddle. I always made him stand a minute before asking him to step out, convinced that his first step might be followed by a rodeo performance. It seemed like the first saddling of the day was the trigger point. After riding him a few minutes or hours, I could resaddle him with no problem whatsoever. It was just one of his quirks. Old habits are hard to break. Even for a horse.

My work schedule allowed me to ride Rocky every morning. I found that even missing a day would cause him to get a little too full of himself. It was a good thing I loved to ride because he loved to go. I didn't want to even think of what he would be like if he stood around for a week. Our daily ritual therefore was a seven to fifteen-mile ride around the low hills to the east of Chino Valley belonging to the Deep Well Ranch. Between the east boundary of Chino and the railroad tracks was a section of pasture that was nearly level except for a ravine running through it. Rocky and I would find a way down into the bottom of this ravine along one of its fingers, then ride until we came to the other end and climbed out or were forced to turn around because of a dead end.

The crevice was as narrow as my stirrups at some points and sometimes twice as deep as we were tall. It was a delightful maze of coyote tracks, rabbit trails and mysterious burrows dug into its banks. Tiny long legged owls would stare at us from the rim after being flushed out of their holes. Rabbits darted from one side of the crevice to another. Topping out we would ride towards the railroad tracks and sometimes see the train heading north towards the ranch where Rocky was born. After waving to the conductor we would continue on our daily adventure.

Once we came across a badger just strolling along. I brought Rocky alongside at a safe distance and the stripe-faced animal turned his head towards us and snarled. Rocky looked at it then paid no more attention to it as if it were a dog. The badger then loped ahead towards a culvert that ran under the railroad tracks and disappeared into it.

Another time we saw a porcupine lumbering down a trail. I thought this was odd due to the lack of anything that resembled a tree for miles in any direction. More often than not we would usually be able to see a small herd of antelope in the distance.

On another foray out into our beloved wilderness we came across a prairie rattler. He had buzzed when we were about ten feet away. Uncle Dale had made it clear that if it were possible to do so, safely exterminate the potential hazard. A bite to the face of a cow or horse could kill. Rocky took notice of the snake but did not panic or jump away. I rode him a safe distance away and hobbled him then came back to find a rock to dispatch the vermin. The problem was, there were no rocks in the area bigger than a pebble. For a state like Arizona that is full of rocks bigger than a space shuttle, I couldn't find one that would do the job. We were on a small hill out on the prairie totally void of rocks. I looked back at Rocky standing calmly waiting for my return and took notice of my saddle's stirrups. They were wrapped thickly with leather and hung like giant bells at Rocky's side. I told the snake to hang around and walked back over to Rocky. I unhooked one of the stirrups and considered the weight of it in my hand. It was heavy enough and if thrown from a short distance might just do the job. It would have to. There was no other suitable object for miles around to use as a weapon. Not even a stick.

The snake coiled up and hissed as I approached. His beady eyes glared at me as if to say, "Hah! What are you going to do? Beat me to death with a stirrup?" "Yes, I am, before you have a chance to cause any more pain or misery." I replied under my nervous breath. Then I did just that.

When I was certain he was dead I pushed his still wiggling head down against the ground and removed it from his body with my tiny pocketknife. I dug a hole with my boot heel and buried it on the side of the hill. Then walked back to Rocky with the remainder of the snake and threw it behind my saddle, tying it securely with a saddle string on either side. It wiggled this way and that as we continued our ride. As we headed back towards civilization I recalled one of our neighbors that had a large litter of children, mostly boys. I reined Rocky into their drive and was quickly surrounded by children ranging in age from toddlers to teens. The older boys quickly spied the carcass draping down from behind my saddle. When their mother came out of the house to say hello, I asked her if her boys could have the beheaded serpent. The younger girls hid behind their mother as their brothers jumped up and down with eagerness. One wanted to make a hat band out of it. Another wanted the bones for a science project coming up at school. The youngest just wanted to save the rattles. The mother gave her permission and I released the still wiggling body into their care. They were delighted as most boys would be. I also thought how delighted my own mother would be that I did not bring it back with me.

Riding Rocky out into the limitless nothingness was always an adventure. I continued his training as we went along, using the tall staghorn cactus to hone his neck reining as Dale had done. We practiced backing up, side passing through a gate, or loping in a serpentine motion changing leads every few yards. Dale had taught me to throw a loop so I sometimes caught a dead cactus skeleton or bush, or tree limb to drag along awhile. Always safety conscience, Dale warned me to never carry a lariat over my shoulder or coil the end of a lead rope around my arm. A horse could get startled and panic, dragging you along with him. Dale had seen such wrecks happen due to carelessness. His seventy-four years accounted for much wisdom.

Rocky and I stopped to drink at a windmill one summer morning on our way home from our daily workout around the Deep Well ranch. As we were enjoying the cold water running from the pipe into the concrete water trough, a small tan pickup drove up. A ruddy faced man stepped out of the truck and walked towards us. I could see that the brand on his custom-made belt buckle matched the brands on the cows in the area. I knew he had to be Harold James, owner of the Deep Well Ranch. He said hello and asked how the water was. I told him "Refreshing", and then I asked if it was okay for me to ride my horse across his property. He told me that it was fine as long as I behaved myself. Then I told him my name, where I lived and that I was putting a lot of 'wet saddle blankets' on the bay horse I was riding.

Over the next few months Mr. James occasionally visited us at my parents' place, bringing me rock salt for Rocky from the Verde Valley or sometimes a bale or two of hay. He noticed my blossoming artistic talent with the western artwork I had hanging at the house and put me to work. He needed several signs for his ranch that stated "Please Close Gate. Behave and Be Welcome." They hung on the ranch gates all around the ranch for decades. Usually a week or two before Christmas I would see his truck stop in front of our place and one of his cowboys would throw a fresh cut Christmas tree over the fence. Once I hollered before they drove away "Harold! Next year keep the Christmas tree and throw the cowboy over the fence!" That really tickled him. Thanks goodness he never did it. I would have been embarrassed beyond words.

Dale had seen fit to introduce me to a lot of the ranchers in the area. Sometimes he would stop by in his little green Datsun and we'd spend the day visiting some of the folks he knew. I had met Delbert Pierce of the Long Meadow when Rocky was there. Galen Neshem was manager of the Indian Rock where I made my dysentery research ride. Dale introduced me to Tom Perkins of the Perkins Ranch, and Billy and Betty Wells of the V7. Dale introduced me to Sis and Sonny Walker down on Ferguson Valley Road. They owned the Bar U Bar. Later on Doug and Sharon Bard would lease the Deep Well Ranch close to my home and I would get to ride with them on gathering days. If there was a cowgirl heaven on earth the good Lord had certainly planted me in the middle of it.

Some of these ranchers let me ride when it was gathering or branding time. Not that I was much help. I was a long way from being a hand, but Rocky and I could cover the country and find cows to bring in. I had the opportunity to ride with Tom Perkins and his family on a roundup at Perkinsville. Nick Perkins still lived there in the white house beneath the cottonwood trees. That same house had been used in the movie 'How the West Was Won' in one of the last scenes. Debbie Reynolds herself might have sat in the same chair I sat in when we came in for lunch that day.

Betty Wells stopped by one day to ask if I could help on a gather and branding. I had a couple days off work so we loaded Rocky into her stock trailer and I spent several days with the Wells family, riding, holding calves down for branding and just trying to be helpful. On the first gather

I rode out with Judy Matli from the Matli Ranch in Williamson Valley. We were deep in the foothills east of Chino riding beneath the high power tension lines to the north. I heard a crackle and Judy exclaimed, "Did you see that? A spark just bounced off my buckle to the metal cap on my saddle horn!" I replied "I heard the crackle but I didn't see it." Judy insisted we ride out from under the power lines. I agreed. Electricity and horses don't blend well.

Later that day we had driven forty of fifty head to the branding corrals. Curt Wells was already there heating up the electric branding irons. Judy Matli, Sharon Wells and I took turns roping and dragging calves to the crew on the ground. Rocky did his job like an old hand. The rope was no longer a threat to him. The bushes and tree limbs and cactus had by now bounced along behind him for many a mile. A calf was just another thing bouncing at the end of the rope. He was more of a cowhorse than I was a cowgirl at this point. I had no clue how to catch a calf by the heels, so I just threw a large enough loop for the calf to jump through, then pulled up the slack to catch his heels. The end result was the same. With the calf caught I turned Rocky towards the branding crew and we delivered the calf. Ears were notched, inoculations given, testicles removed and an enormous V7 was burned down their left hind leg. I think the brand was large enough to spot from an airplane. There would be no mistaking the Wells Ranch cattle.

Rocky and I spent the summer riding all over and around the Chino Basin. We climbed Table Mountain numerous times, visited the Verde River, rode out along the abandoned narrow gauge railroad tracks to the east, and to Mint Wash on the west. If the wind was right and the hills sufficient to give us cover we'd sneak up on a herd of antelope and come over the last hill at a run. It was never a contest. I could almost hear the antelope laughing as they disappeared over the next hill before we'd made it to where they had just been.

On one of our many visits to the Verde River, I varied our route and Rocky and I stumbled upon a place that had been scooped out on the side of a hill that was covered with red rocks. Later I relayed the story about the place and was told it was an old pipestone quarry. The native Indians used this type of red soapstone to carve their peace pipes out of. Hence the name pipestone. The only other place I know of in the lower forty-eight that the rock is found is in Minnesota. Some of the pueblo tribes make red jewelry out of it and carved fetishes.

As it happens in cow country there were remains of dead cattle on the high prairie that had died from lightning or calving or other natural causes. Ranchers do a wonderful job of caring for their herds in the best possible way but occasionally one would be found dead. This was always

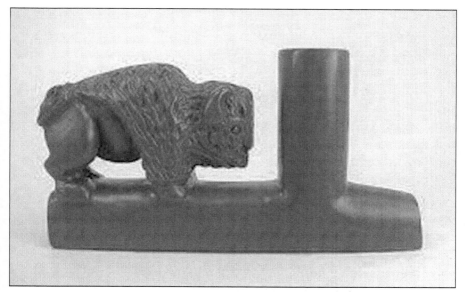

Carved pipestone.

a tragedy and financial loss for a rancher but it comes with the territory. For me however it was a puzzle. Literally. As a budding artist I would study the cows anatomy by piecing the scattered bones back together. Mysteriously skeletons were reassembled in the hills around Chino Valley. No longer strewn about by coyotes or vultures, the skeletons could now be found galloping, jumping or trotting flat against the ground depending how I positioned the legs.

Once Rocky and I came across the carcass of a sorrel horse at the north end of town. Lightning had not killed this one. Its hind legs were tangled tightly in a web of barbed wire. Wire was looped around its body and front legs. It had been a slow and painful death. I could still see cuts along the now dried hide. The flesh had pulled back away from its lips and I could tell from the teeth that it was not an old horse nor a young one. The sight sickened me and I turned Rocky away and rode quietly home.

It had been nearly a year since I had brought Rocky home from the

Del Rio Ranch. After a rough start he had finally traded his old habits for new ones. Rocky was never a 'pocket pet' type of horse. He was in his thirties before he would come up to me to be petted or scratched. I think that in his heart he would have preferred to live wild out in the hills. Like the story of Coaly-Bay by Ernest Seton, Rocky would have been content to live out his life in the canyons of the Verde far away from man. But because of my entering his life the total opposite was about to happen.

My parents had made the decision to return to Southern California for the winter in order to finish some business and I was informed I would be going with them. This was devastating news for me. After working with Rocky so many hours to give him a good foundation I was going to have to leave him behind or find a way to move him. We had no trailer and I didn't have the money to buy one. I couldn't think of anyone that would loan us one and there were none available to rent. Seeing my anguish my dad came up with an idea. Dale had transported Rocky in the back of his Datsun pickup in a box he had built that was similar to what the airlines use. It was secured to the vehicle and Dale used it to transport his cow horse from one area to another. It had a ramp for the horse to walk up and the entire top was open like a stock trailer. It wasn't pretty but it worked. Dad would build one for Rocky in the back of his 1960 Ford 150.

Early one morning I led Rocky to the ramp at the back of dad's green truck and after a moment's hesitation, Rocky scrambled up. We were on our way. As I look back on this adventure I shudder with trepidation at how this three hundred sixty-mile trip could have turned out badly. Rocky was a horse with horse sense though and rode like a champ. Many prayers accompanied us that day.

I had to laugh when we drove under the first overpass as Rocky suddenly ducked his head as if he was going to hit it. He did this at every over pass and there were plenty of them. We drove down the winding White Spar Road out of Prescott and I prayed Rocky wouldn't get carsick. His head and neck hung out over the top of the cab and if I turned to look through the rear window I could see his knees behind the wood slats. We drove down Yarnell Hill slowly. Rocky's view from the top must have been outstanding. A thousand feet below miles of desert floor spread out below him to the south and west. This was his first time 'off the farm' so to speak. I wondered if he ever comprehended how big the world was that he lived in. Each time we stopped I crawled up to offer him water and a few bites of hay. Traveling at a maximum speed of fifty-five miles per hour it took over six hours to reach our destination. I'm sure Rocky was happier than I was when we backed him down the ramp at Fred Yingst's place on the outskirts of Ontario. The other horses nickered hello and Rocky responded with a robust call of his own as if to say "Thanks goodness I made it here alive!"

Rocky had no idea where he had landed but he was about to find out. If there was a location as inhospitable for a half-broke cowhorse fresh off the range as this place was, I couldn't imagine it. Rocky was about to experience a severe culture shock. Fred directed me to Rocky's new corral. I led him through the gate and turned him loose. He trotted over to sniff noses with another horse in an adjoining pen then rolled in the dirt and took in his surroundings.

The front of the property faced Holt Boulevard, a main thoroughfare between Ontario and the inland empire. Semi trucks and heavy traffic drove day and night along this four-lane access to the I-10 freeway a half mile away. A few hundred yards to the east was the main entrance to the Ontario International Airport. It was located directly south of Holt Boulevard extending a mile or more both directions. The only thing that separated Rocky's back fence from the airport was a narrow slice of land just wide enough for a pair of tracks belonging to the Atchison, Topeka and Santa Fe Railroad. It was a good thing Rocky lacked opposing thumbs as I do believe he would have shot himself to escape this black hole of wild chaos he had fallen into. There was nowhere to run. There was no escape. He was surrounded by planes, trains and automobiles almost close enough for him to touch.

The only saving aspect of this cow pony torture center was the vineyards. Across Holt was an abandoned vineyard a half mile wide. Next to it was another, and another. These dried up vineyards checker-boarded together into an escape route that led all the way to the foothills of Mt. Baldy. Sometimes the old vineyards had been replaced with new ones or orange groves but they were still open enough for riding. From the back of a horse the orange citrus was easy to reach, juicy and delicious on a warm southern California day. Grapes also disappeared occasionally as we rode along. It was like riding along in the garden of Eden. I wish I could say how much I loved it but I didn't. I counted the days, aching to return to my wild Arizona.

I took a job with a horse trader named Don White. After feeding in the morning I would saddle up and ride the string of horses he had returned from Utah with. He sold broke horses to the city folk and it was my job to exercise them. The horses arrived in all sizes, colors and breeds. Don showed me how to clip the horses to take the 'rough' off. We removed the auction tags and brushed the horses down. After a few months I moved Rocky there so I could spend more time with him. One time Don returned with a load of horses and a gorgeous sorrel overo paint gelding came off the truck. After riding him Don offered to trade him for Rocky straight across. The paint gelding was very well broke and a pleasure to ride. Something stopped me from making the trade. I think it was my concern for Rocky and fear that his rough spots that still needed to be worked out would end him up in a slaughterhouse. I had become fond of the ornery little bay and in my mind I wasn't ready to part with him. Not even for a push button Paint.

I enrolled in some animal science classes at Mt. Sac College for the fall. Several of my classmates invited me to bring my horse and ride with them on their annual trail ride. When I questioned them on the location and duration I was informed we would be riding in the hills behind the college, possibly traveling two miles or more and back. I would have enjoyed having a group of my peers to ride with, but it would have taken longer to get Rocky hauled there than the ride would last, so I declined. Arizona still was beckoning me with its smog free wilderness.

Spring couldn't arrive fast enough. In April dad put the horse containment unit back in the truck and early the next morning we drove down to pick up Rocky. It wasn't even daylight yet when I led him to the back of the truck. Rocky took one look at the contraption and froze. He wasn't about to climb back into that thing. We coaxed and offered food but he wouldn't budge. It would have been easier to push a marshmallow into a piggy bank. Finally dad said "Give him to me." My dad took the lead rope and walked Rocky away a few steps. Then he whispered something into Rocky's ear. When they came back to the truck a minute later Rocky scrambled right up the ramp into the truck. As we headed east onto the I-10 freeway I asked my dad "What did you say to him to get him to go into the truck?" Dad smiled and said, "I told him now Rocky, you need to get into the truck. We're going to take you back to Arizona!"

It felt so good to be back in the mountains. Rocky and I picked up where we had left off. He had gotten to the point I trusted him enough to discontinue the sideline. He still did his stiff-legged dance as I led him out but I just told him what foolishness it was and that he'd better save his energy for the day's ride.

One morning I caught Rocky a little earlier than usual, saddled up and headed west towards Table Mountain. The warm spring sun had barely begun to peak over Mingus Mountain as we passed the cemetery on Road Two South. I could begin to feel its warmth on my back by the time we reached the foothills. The early morning's coolness has faded as I directed Rocky between the pinyon trees and scrub oak. We were climbing. The oak brush and trees began getting thicker and then without warning we found ourselves in a small level clearing.

The early morning sun was now warming the ground and the vegetation all around us. The morning breeze was an ambrosia of warmed earth, pine, oak, sumac, and blossoms from some unseen wildflowers. I heard a Mexican Jay squawk at our intrusion. Quail whistled from their hiding places in the brush. A rock squirrel chirped in the distance. It seemed as though the place where we found ourselves was almost enchanted. I held Rocky still as my senses awakened to experience the phenomena. All the essence of primeval Arizona had chosen this small spot to converge. I sat still on my horse taking in slow deep breaths of the warm mountain air. Rocky's scent mingled through to blend with the others. It felt as if we had walked into the pages of an old Zane Grey novel, expecting to be transformed into one of the characters he created. Rocky patiently stood while I sat mesmerized by the moment. After a short time I reluctantly touched my heels to his side and we continued on. I had never experienced anything like this before, or since.

On Tuesdays I would have Rocky jump in the back of dad's pickup and we would drive the ten miles or so to the Nelson Livestock auction near the Prescott Airport. They had offered me a job working pens on sale day. Rocky and I would push the cattle one at a time or in groups to their appointed pens after they had been sold in the ring. Rocky loved his job. For our days labor I would receive a hamburger from the concession trailer and fifteen dollars. To me it was a dream job and Rocky enjoyed it too.

Rocky and I covered a lot of miles that summer. Doug Bard and his wife Sharon had leased part of the Deep Well Ranch from Harold James and moved into a house just down the road from us. They invited me to 'go along for the ride' on many occasions. One of the most memorable for me was the day Doug's son Travis rode with us. He was the epitome of young cow-boyhood sitting astride his old sorrel gelding named Okie. His over sized black cowboy hat spread wide across his head and shaded his freckled face. He reminded me of one of the characters from the John Wayne movie "The Cowboys". From beneath the wide brim I could see his dark eyes sparkle. His grin showed that he had two brand new eyeteeth that were just beginning to fill in. I teased him about them saying "Travis, How are you ever going to eat any sweet corn on the cob this summer if you don't have any teeth?" Travis solemnly replied, "Miss Marilyn, I can eat sweet corn just fine!"

Travis' short legs barely reached down to the center of old Okie's belly. On the back of his small cowboy boots was a well-used set of little spurs. In his right hand he carried a lariat. As we rode along Travis would swing the rope into a big loop and rope anything growing up out of the ground. He entertained himself by seeing which various forms of vegetation he could pop out of the ground or drag along until the rope lost its grip. Our destination that summer day was the Deep Well Ranch headquarters several miles away. Doug and Travis rode side by side. Vern Thompson and I rode further apart giving the young roper plenty of room to practice his roping skills.

"Travis" I teased again. "How is it someone as short as you can ride so tall in the saddle?" He'd just grin showing his new front teeth again. At one point Travis laid his loop over a cactus a bit larger than the ones he'd been roping. He dallied the rope around his saddle horn and his gelding kept plodding forward. This time however the cactus didn't let go of the rope. I watched Travis' father, Doug, quietly direct his gray gelding Dollar away from his boy. The rope stretched and tightened until the cactus suddenly popped out of the ground. The rope snapped back like a rubber band bringing the cactus with it and slapped the gelding on his big belly just behind the stirrups. The gelding jumped sideways but the young cowboy kept his seat. The cactus was stuck to Okie right behind Travis' boot. The gelding jumped again and all but two chunks of cactus fell to the ground. Doug came to his sons rescue and scraped the remaining cactus from the horse's side with his coiled lariat. "Son" Doug said, "If you keep roping cactus you're going to get your hands full of needles that have gotten stuck in your rope. You were lucky this time. Next time it might snap back and hit you in the back of your head. And if you're on another horse he might not be so forgiving as Okie." With age comes wisdom and I'm sure the rancher shared it with his son on many occasions. Common sense is a prerequisite to being a cowboy or a rancher.

On one occasion I gathered up a bunch of youngsters from town and we rode out across the valley to the foothills of Mingus Mountain. Tom Perkins had invited us to come play cowboy for the day and help him move a herd closer to town. It was about a twelve-mile ride to where we caught up with Tom and his family. By noon the cattle had been gathered. We stopped and were fed lunch out of the back of an old station wagon. Refreshed, the group of kids and I followed the cattle back towards Chino along the old narrow gauge bed. It was a typical hot Arizona afternoon. We rode back and forth behind the cattle like buzzing bees. There were five or six of us in the group that day. I remember Coy and Troy Baker were there riding tall on their ponies. It was the first cattle drive for all of them and they enjoyed every dust-covered mile of it.

From our position we could see all the way to Prescott some twenty miles away. The hot valley floor we rode on was spread out and barren to the west and south. The foothills of the Verde River flanked us on the north. Across the valley we could see dust devils swirling here and there in the distance. A really big one could be watched for several minutes before it lost its power and disappeared into the blue sky. Half way back to our destination I began to watch a dust devil approach from the southwest. It followed along the dry Granite Creek bed throwing tumbleweeds far into the air and swirling dirt and brush along as it went. I wondered what the cattle would do if a really big one hit the herd. It wasn't long before I would find out.

It seemed our cattle were heading right into it. Ten minutes later the dust devil had grown to what must have been an F5. It was a half-mile wide and blowing like a banshee. It hit the narrow gauge exactly where the cattle were walking. Dirt, sand, tumbleweeds, leaves, and dried grass blew around and through us with the ferocity of a tornado. I watched huge tumbleweeds bounce off the backs of the Hereford cows in front of me. The dirt was so thick I could not see the roadbed beneath me. Flying sticks hit Rocky on his legs and to his credit he calmly continued on. Being in the elements all his life he had learned to deal with them. I covered my face with my arm to protect it from the stinging sand and squinted my eyes as tight as I could. And then, it was gone. I watched it blow off to the northwest and slowly fade into the foothills. The cows were still plodding down the road. All hands were accounted for and still moving in the right direction. Just another day in paradise.

My first overnight ride with Rocky that summer was in the middle of monsoon season. Another Chino Valley girl and I took off towards Williamson Valley on our horses with the intent of staying the night in a hay shack in the foothills west of Chino that belonged to Everette Brisedine. Our saddlebags were packed tight with necessities like oranges, sandwiches and Big Hunk candy bars. I had put my canteen in the freezer the night before so I could sip ice cold water all day.

The summer day started off as usual. Hot and dry. By midday the small popcorn shaped clouds grew large and started to turn dark. We had made our way to Williamson Valley Road and were happily riding the back country of the Cooper-Morgan Ranch when the first cool breeze hit us. Lightning cracked a few miles away and we started looking for shelter. The pasture we were riding in led us down to a wash that went under the two-lane blacktop road to the west. The concrete sided underpass was tall enough for us to ride our horses into. The rain started to pour as we made for cover and we found ourselves drenched to the skin before we reached the shelter. The horses were happy to be out of the pelting rain. Lightning cracked and thunder rolled over us. I could taste the electricity in the air. Rocky stood calmly as my friend's horse jumped at the boom of lightning. As it goes with Arizona summer thunderstorms it slacked off in a short while and I suggested we get out of the low spot in the event of a flash flood.

The late afternoon sun dried us off as we rode. We had traveled as far as Inscription Canyon on the old Morgan Ranch. As evening fell we headed back towards the hay shed in the foothills west of Chino. There was a two-acre pasture fenced off for the horses to spend the night in with plenty of grass to eat. A water trough for the range cattle was full if the horses needed a drink. We packed our saddles into the shed and cleared a small area of the grass hay that was strewn across the floor. I put down a thick saddle pad for my bed and turned my saddle fleece side up for my pillow. My Navajo blanket would be my cover. I was ready for bed. We had opened a can of pork and beans and heated it up on a small fire. The inside of the shed was cozy enough. It never occurred to me that things that slither might have been sharing the room with us. As we devoured the can of delicious half warmed beans I savored their flavor along with my surroundings. What I was tasting was freedom. I had spent the day riding across the open range, choosing any direction to go that my heart desired. My horse Rocky had given me the ability to ride as far as yearned to go. I dozed off to sleep contemplating what it would be like to ride Rocky to the many unexplored places I had seen and beyond. It was the best of times.

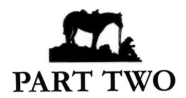

PART TWO

THE DARK AGES

Growing up in a Christian home I heard the preacher at church speak about a horrible time in the future called the Tribulation Period. He said it would last seven years and then went on to describe some of the unspeakable conditions that would occur. The images he brought forth were horrid, dreadful and appalling. I couldn't imagine anyone surviving such an ordeal. He spoke of brutality, murder, hatred, daughters against mothers, fathers against their children, homelessness, lack of food, searing heat, darkness, affliction, betrayal, deception and desolation. This Tribulation began for me in 1975 and ended in 1989. It was in fact two Tribulations Periods back to back. A bad marriage.

I had met a young man that I thought would be a good mate. Except for his lack of work ethic, laziness, poor hygiene, cruelty, paranoia, bitterness, compulsive lying, violence, narcissism, and total lack of morals we had a lot in common. He had a horse. I had a horse. He told me he was going to own his own ranch someday. I was smitten. What he failed to mention was that he would be stealing the cows. These were just a few things that were not revealed prior to wedlock.

Rocky however seemed to understand this persons persona right from the start. Because I had to spend a week back in California with my mother to prepare for the wedding I asked my 'husband to be' to do one thing for me while I was away. I wanted him to continue riding Rocky for me each day while I was gone. I did not believe the task to be difficult for him as he had plenty of time in the afternoon and was a rider and capable to saddle Rocky and complete the task. To make things less difficult I brought Rocky over to his parent's home where he lived to make it more convenient.

Seven days later I returned. All I had to do was look at my fiancée to understand what happened and it wasn't good. He looked up at me sheepishly from his parent's sofa, bloodied, bruised, scraped and bandaged. He could barely get up. "Was there a problem?" I asked, knowing the evidence pointed to the fact that he had not ridden Rocky daily as per my request. He confessed he had waited till the day before my return to ride him. Then told me the order of events that led to his injuries.

He had saddled Rocky and rode out the driveway with his younger brother. At the corner they decided to race down the dirt road so he kicked Rocky into a gallop. Rocky started bucking and headed into the bar ditch alongside the road where the telephone pole was. Rocky made a beeline right for it, head down and cranking hard. Then he veered to the right slamming my beloved fiancee against the pole and continued bucking down the road. Still in the saddle my future husband lasted only a jump or two then hit the hard ground. Rocky wasn't done with him yet however. His unseated rider's boot was caught in the stirrup and Rocky had no intention of slowing down. Rocky dragged him kicking and bucking another fifty yards down the road. Finally his victim's foot slipped out of the stirrup to leave him groaning in the dirt and dried tumbleweeds at the side of the road.

My feelings were mixed with compassion for the damages my horse had done to my fiancee and confusion as to why he had not followed through with my request. My judgment had been disregarded and request ignored resulting in a wreck. Not a good way to begin a marriage. This incident brought up a series of issues I should not have ignored. My fiancee had shown he was unreliable. Had he honored my request most likely the episode would have been avoided. And now I was concerned that all my work with Rocky had been thrown out the window. As the saying goes, 'Fools rush in where angels fear to tread'. So I saddled Rocky the next day and with much trepidation, climbed aboard.

Same old Rocky! We rode to Table Mountain as if nothing had happened. Fact is Rocky never bucked with me again, ever. He was my partner and as far as I was concerned a very well broke horse. He did however take delight in bucking off quite a few people during the next thirty years. I just wasn't one of them. Like Hannibal Lector, he preferred to condemn the 'free-range' rude. As it turned out they were mostly relatives of my new husband.

Eight weeks after our wedding my spouse was fired from his job. Because we lived with his parents he never felt the need to seek new employment after that.. His parents provided us with a roof over our heads, (we lived in their old barn), and groceries (provided to them by the U.S. taxpayer). His father received a monthly check from Uncle Sam. Optimistic as always I considered our situation a temporary condition. This temporary condition lasted through the two Tribulation Periods previously mentioned.

My father suggested we take a trip to visit my brother Ken near Dimmit, Texas. There was work available there. Ken was an Ag pilot and assured us that jobs were available with many of the huge farms in the area. My father even offered to take us there to check it out. We were living with my in-laws at this time, where 'unreliability' was a family trait. The day before we left I filled the water tank and moved some hay close to the feeder where Rocky would be while we were gone. He shared a large pasture with two white donkeys, a pony and another horse. The pasture had been overgrazed for years. The donkeys had even dug up the roots of what was left and ate that too. There was a sloppily made catch pen that the animals came into each day for food and water. The three strands of barbed wire looped lazily from post to post to make the enclosure. Inside was the water tank. I was content that there would be plenty of water to last the few days we would be gone. My husband's family would throw hay over the fence for the animals.

Halfway into the trip I started feeling uneasy. We had driven straight through the night and arrived early the next morning. Although I enjoyed seeing my brother and his family I was impatient to get back to Rocky. Something was wrong. I had never been impressed with how my father-in-law cared for his livestock and now Rocky was under his care. The silage pit on his property was filled with the carcasses of their deceased animals. Calves that died of scours, cows from bloat, cats that the grandpa had shot just for fun, leftover animal parts from butchering, and horses. It seemed as though sooner or later all the horses they owned ended up in the pit. Colic killed most of them. The hay of choice for those poor beasts was Bermuda straw. It was the cheapest thing you could buy. The only time I ever saw alfalfa get fed was when two bales fell off a truck on the road in front of their place. They were quickly procured and disposed of into the mouths of hungry livestock.

We had been gone six days. As soon as we drove past the pasture I felt sick. Rocky and the other horse were standing close to the barbed wire enclosure looking thin and drawn. I jumped out of the truck nearly before it stopped. The donkeys and pony were in the small enclosure and the gate was closed. Uneaten hay was scattered around. Rocky and the other horse had been locked out, away from the feed and the water tank. Needless to say I was livid. The two horses looked as though they hadn't had any water or feed since we left. I ran to the gate and both horses met me there making straight for the water tank. Running for halters and lead ropes I caught them to keep them from drinking too much too fast.

It was all I could do to keep from blasting into my in-laws for their negligence. Apparently one of their cows escaped and they finally trapped her in the small pen. When they closed the gate to catch her they forgot to reopen it again. All the animals had been trapped outside but the donkeys and pony wormed their way through the loose barbed wire to get to the water. The horses couldn't. It had been four days. It was a miracle that Rocky and the other survived. My respect for this family had grown thin.

The decision was made to relocate to Texas. I was glad to get away from my in-laws. My brother would let us double up with him for awhile until my husband found work. Our only means of transportation was an old two-ton flatbed truck with solid sides. We would load all our worldly belongings into the bed, including Rocky and the two donkeys. We looked like something right out of the Grapes of Wrath as we drove the thousand miles. Rocky stood at the front of the truck bed with a white donkey on each side. There was a pull up four-foot wide gate on the left side of the old truck. If we drove into a bar ditch on that side it would be a small jump for the horse and donkeys to make into or out of the bed of the truck. Rocky was used to hopping into my dad's pickup and hardly hesitated. The donkeys would go anywhere food was available. Behind the animals two two-by-fours across the truck bed separated them from our few belongings.

We drove nearly non-stop along I-40. Rocky and the two donkeys, Speck and Sadie had a front row seat over the cab of the truck through the Land of Enchantment and on to the unending plains of Texas. By the time we arrived my dear brother had found a wonderful pasture to put Rocky and his friends in. It was a low spot on the endless prairie that was still covered with the original grasses before the plows came. A tiny creek ran through the bottom. It was owned by a friend from their church and consisted of several hundred acres. There would be no charge for board. They were happy to have the area mowed and Rocky and the white long-eared twins could stay as long as needed. We found a hill to pull the truck next to and unloaded our weary passengers. After releasing them into their new home all three dropped to roll and galloped off to an adjacent rise, then heads went down to the grass and only came up occasionally to scan their new domain.

My husband's first job only lasted a couple of weeks. Much to my delight the next job came with a house! The beautiful brick house sat in a cul-de-sac right next to the farmers wheat field where he would be working. I spent the weekend moving in and getting our few things sorted out. At the end of the week he got fired again. I never knew why. But we had to move again. Then he found a job at a feedlot outside the town of Muleshoe. We found a tiny white house a mile down the road from the feedlot and rented it. There still was no place to keep Rocky so he stayed out on the pasture. A few days later we were told he could be kept and used at the feedlot. I had hired on as a silage truck driver at the same place. It would be good to have Rocky close again and I enjoyed my daily routine of feeding the cattle.

Rocky had to earn his keep. He was used to move cattle and work the pens. On occasion he was taken to the mile square adjacent pasture to rope and tend sick cattle. Sometimes I would ride him when I was done feeding the cattle but most of the time my husband rode him. Rocky bloomed in this environment. He knew what his purpose was and that was to work those cows. It was a thing of beauty to watch him cut cattle out of the group. Unlike the cutting horse classes where horses back away from the cow to give a good show, Rocky was serious and meant business. Once you set him on a cow, you were just along for the ride. He would have made his daddy Sut Breeze proud. They had the same work ethic, which meant you had better hold onto your hat. Rocky once pushed a steer into the fence and the steer jumped over it. It was all his rider could do to hold Rocky back from going over the fence after him. He was a fine cow pony.

It had only been a couple of months when my spouse came in from work early to announce that he'd quit, and that he told our boss I'd quit too. I really enjoyed working there. It was an outdoor job and I liked to feed the cattle with the Ensilmixer. It was upsetting to find myself unemployed, but by now I had figured out my spouse had a tendency to be controlling and it was easier to go along that stir his anger. In a matter of days the donkeys and Rocky and I were back in the truck heading towards Arizona and his parents.

We made it almost as far as Grants, New Mexico when the truck quit running. We were stranded alongside I-40 with very little money and three animals stuck in the truck with no way to unload them. Some locals offered to tow the truck to a mechanic and they knew someone who could put Rocky and the donkeys up for the night. After finally unloading them and getting them into a corral we walked over to a rest area along I-40 and slept on a concrete slab near a picnic table. The next morning the truck problem was discovered and easily fixed. I paid the man who had kept Rocky and the donkeys overnight with the last few dollars in my pocket. I was grateful they could be in a place where they had room to move around and thought they had probably slept better than I did. We loaded Rocky, Speck and Sadie back into the green truck and continued west.

A few weeks after moving back in with my spouses parents a job became available at the Z3 Ranch near Skull Valley. Ray Contreras was the ranch manager there. The salary wasn't much but the job came with a tiny mobile home at the ranch. I was beginning to have nightmares about living with my in-laws forever and much relieved when we moved to the Z3. Perhaps now we could settle into something more permanent. I yearned for some stability for myself and the baby I now carried. Rocky was under the not so watchful eye of my father-in-law again. This situation was not what I wanted but until I could get permission to bring him to the Z3 I had no other option.

At the end of two months my husband was fired once again. I was devastated. The Z3 was a beautiful ranch near Sheridan Mountain just a few miles west of Skull Valley. Even living in that tiny trailer I could have been happy there for forty years. But now we had to move again, back in with his parents, of course. This time our residence would be the camper that had been removed from a pickup that was set on the ground just outside the backdoor of his parents house. The only upside was that I would be back there to care for Rocky.

Four days after the baby was born I found myself living in an eight dollar a night motel room in Flagstaff. Friction between my parents and my spouse caused him to isolate me from them even more than before. My husband had already informed me that I was not to call them, and visits were totally out of the question. I sat alone with a newborn in the motel room with no money or food while he looked for work. A small company that worked on and installed sewer lines hired him and we were able to rent a trailer from one of their relatives. No place for horses there or within a reasonable distance.

Rocky would have to stay with the in-laws for the time being. I prayed he would be taken care of. The corrals for their livestock were dilapidated. They were built mostly of slabs of long splintered boards held together with baling wire. Years and years of manure from the cattle, goats and horses accumulated in them. Huge rusted long nails stuck out everywhere. The entire property was covered with trash and junk, dead automobiles and garbage. Except for a few elms most of the trees were dead, standing as sentries around a black hole of debris.

Six weeks into the job we moved again. My spouse was allergic to paying rent and besides, the job they would be working at for the next month or so was at the Grand Canyon. An old camp trailer near the job was available so we packed up our few things and went to the Canyon. I was willing to put up with nearly anything for the sake of employment. By the time we arrived the camp trailer had been occupied. We therefore stayed in a two-man tent out in the forest with our two-month-old baby. Incredibly I found the next four weeks to be wonderful. I spent the days packing my baby around the south rim of the Grand Canyon. If I could have only found a place to keep Rocky near me I would have literally been a happy camper. I found the employee showers and cafeteria. I visited the shops and walked along the rim with the tourists. My only concern was that I had to be back at the tent before my husband returned or there would be consequences.

On weekends we would always drive back to visit my husband's parents. Visits to my parents were not allowed even though they were just a few miles away. While my in-laws doted over our new little girl, I would catch Rocky, saddle up and head for the hills. I preferred to ride alone. Rocky was my sanctuary. My husband seldom let me out of his sight but on Rocky I could escape if only for a few hours.

When he quit this job after a month we once again moved back in with his parents. He had decided to make his fortune by cutting and selling firewood. He would of course require my presence and assistance. I was expected to go out to the forest each time he went to load the days wood into the trailer. I actually liked being out in the woods. It was away from his family and I really didn't mind helping to make a living. I felt like Br'er Rabbit being thrown into the briar patch. I was comfortable in the wilderness. And by my contributing to the family income, I felt guilt-

1978 Friendly Pines N.A.T.R.C. Ride. Spruce Mountain.

less in asking to spend a few dollars for an entry fee to take Rocky to an N.A.T.R.C. sanctioned ride.

My request was granted and I sent the thirty-five dollars out in the mail. The first ride was in Wickenburg and would be fifty miles long. Rocky and I had never done any competition of any kind. This would be an adventure. We were assigned a number and pointed down a trail marked with ribbons. We rode around Vulture Peak and ended up back at the ranch we had left earlier that morning after covering thirty-five miles. The next morning we rode the last fifteen. At one point along the trail two judges were hidden in the brush above a rough rocky climb. I overheard one say to the other, "Watch this horse climb through these rocks!" The comment made my day. Rocky never broke a sweat on that ride. He was probably wondering where the cattle were. That evening they gave us a ribbon. Not the first place, but still a high spot in the group of riders that had participated.

Later that summer we rode in the Friendly Pines sponsored fifty-mile N.A.T.R.C. ride near Prescott, Arizona. The third and last one we did was the Buttercup Memorial near Lake Mary south of Flagstaff. A few days before I left I got a call from my mom. My husband glared at me as I reached for the phone. She informed me that Dale Girdner had died and that his funeral would be on Saturday. That year at the Prescott Frontier Days Rodeo they had a moment of silence prior to each performance in honor of Dale Girdner, the kindly old rancher that took pity on a young woman and her outlaw horse. He was well known and respected throughout Yavapai County and the Verde Valley.

A miracle finally happened! My spouse had found gainful employment. My prayers had been answered and I hoped to now have a somewhat stable life. We rented a forty-acre pasture to keep Rocky and our livestock in for fifty dollars a month. It was located in Chino at the southeast corner of Road Two South and One West. There was an old wooden barn in its center and the main irrigation ditch for Chino Valley ran through it. It had not been grazed for years and had abundant grass. Rocky loved it. During the heat of the day he could walk down into the cool irrigation ditch and graze along its banks at eye level, letting the cool water from Watson Lake flow around his legs. Our other horses followed his lead and spent the summer days in their refreshing horse spa.

My spouse's job schedule gave him every other day off from work and sometimes three or four days off in a row. He began buying and selling a few horses in the hopes of making a profit. Because of his hot temper it was unbearable to watch him work those poor animals. I despised myself for not doing something to stop him, but I was more afraid he would turn his anger towards me, or Rocky. I felt helpless.

Once I watched in horror as he beat a young mare through a wooden corral fence with his bare hands. She was a pretty sorrel stocking legged mare that ended up in the possession of my friend Lavon Cooper. She loved that little mare and kept her at her home opposite from the old Chino High School. Lavon owned the Chino Valley Grain feed store before it became Olsen's. When I went in for hay one time she told me about her new stocking legged mare that she had named Velvet. She was a calm, quiet mare. A pleasure to ride. Except for one incident when she rode her past an old wood board corral. Lavon said she couldn't get Velvet to go near it and finally gave it a wide berth. The mare was terrified of it. Ashamed, I said nothing.

Another occasion my mate beat a bay mare into the ground with a heavy chain. I cringed in terror as I knew what those horses were going through. His beatings were not just reserved for our horses or dogs.

That September we had gone to the Yavapai County Fair so we could help my father-in-law prepare his dairy cows for the show. While there I spoke with another man showing his livestock whom my husband didn't like. On the drive home he went into a jealous rage. Because he was driving he could only strike at me with his right arm. I pushed myself as close to the far door as possible to escape his fist. At a stop sign he pulled out his 38-caliber pistol and leaned over, putting the barrel on my left temple. "I ought to kill you right here!" he growled. I waited for the flash, frozen in fear. Mercifully a car pulled up behind us and he lowered the gun and drove on. It was only a few weeks later during one of his tantrums he grabbed a rifle and stomped out into the back yard. He shot and killed two of his own dogs to prove his point. I got the message. My life, my daughter, my horse and anyone I loved were at risk. I made a decision to sell Rocky. It wasn't safe for him.

I put an ad in the local paper and before long an older married couple came out to try him. They wanted a trail horse for the wife. She took him out for a few minutes and said they'd discuss it and call me back. Later that evening they called and said that they wanted to buy him. I cringed. Something in me told me to back out. "I'm sorry" I told her. "I've changed my mind. I don't want to sell him." She said she understood and that I should give her a call if something changed. Something needed to change. I was living in terror, walking on eggshells in fear of saying or doing something that would send the unstable person I was married to into a violent frenzy.

The gainful employment only lasted a few months. Once again we moved back in with his parents. This time however was short lived as they sold their property and moved to Texas. We ended up living instead with his grandmother in her tiny eight foot wide trailer. With not much else to do my spouse found entertainment in illegal activities. Within a short while, with the threat of his being arrested for arson as well as cattle rustling we followed his mom and dad to Texas. This time Rocky rode to Texas in his parents open top stock trailer . It was a long drive to his parent's place just outside of Carlton, Texas. We arrived around midnight after being on the road for over thirty hours. The horses had not been out of the trailer for the entire time. I unloaded Rocky and the mare that was with him and put them in the first empty corral I could find, then threw them the last of the hay we had brought with us. I was exhausted as much as the horses and looked forward to some much-needed rest. I walked into the house to discover no one had thought to provide us a place to sleep. My little girls were laid end to end on the old sofa and I crumpled down next to them on the floor. With no blanket or pillow I fell asleep thinking about how things could have been worse as visions of sleeping on the concrete alongside I-40 danced in my head.

At four a.m. the father of this domestic disaster came into the kitchen which adjoined the living room and began his day. The perpetual coffeepot was restarted and the ensuing clink of his spoon against his cup began. He was the new proud owner of a real dairy and had to rise early to milk the cows. For some reason the government had loaned him a ridiculous sum to purchase this existing farm where we now all resided. It came with a wonderful producing herd of about 90 Holstein cows which were soon sold and replaced with less efficient Jerseys. He claimed the loss of their milk volume would be made up by the higher butterfat content of the smaller cows. After seeing his previous dairy management techniques at the old place I wondered how long this fiasco would last. None of his three lazy sons would offer to help. It would not take long for the debris and clutter to accumulate. Things would fall apart and not be repaired or replaced. My heart went out to the poor cows that would be the ones to suffer the most.

Having been raised on an award-winning dairy in Chino, California I had a good idea of how things operated. In the herd of five hundred my father would occasionally have to treat one cow for mastitis. Here, within a few months it had spread to at least thirty cows. The somatic cell count was over the moon. It all boiled down to filthy practices before and during milking. Before long this formally normal family farm had lost its Grade A rating and was issued a D rating. 'For animal consumption only'. The concrete slab floor of the holding pen the cows stood in prior to milking was belly deep in their own manure. Their udders drug through the green slime as they slowly moved towards the milking parlor entrance. Once I spent an hour shoveling and washing it down to expose the concrete below only to get chastised for doing so. My father-in-laws excuse was that a cow might slip and break a leg on the concrete. The deep manure would keep that from happening. He must have thought having cows with mastitis was better.

During the two years we were there my parents came to visit once. They only stayed a few hours. My dad saw one of the cows barely alive with bluebag, her body emaciated and told me that she should have been mercifully sent to the canners a month earlier. She lived less than a week, half her udder rotted away. Since my in-laws had acquired the farm the whole place had begun to rot away. They managed with the help of their never ending government check to hang on to the place for four years. Finally unable to keep up with the huge farm loan and their local feed bill amassing to over fifty thousand dollars they filed bankruptcy and walked away. The property and cattle were repossessed. The surviving cattle sold at auction.

During the two years we stayed with them I seldom rode Rocky off the farm. There was no open country in which to ride. Everything was fenced in and the only place to ride was alongside the little farm roads or in someone's field. I missed the wide-open spaces of Arizona. Feeling more trapped than ever I started suggesting how nice it would be to go back home to my beloved Arizona. The only thing holding us was the uncut umbilical cord from my spouse to his parents. I ached to run away. Our only vehicle had quit running thanks to the lack of oil in the crankcase. I was now afoot except for Rocky. If it had not been for my two precious daughters, I would have saddled up in the middle of the night and slipped off into the west.

An unexpected check arrived in the mail early in 1983 from an insurance company for a dog bite my oldest had received. It wasn't a life-changing amount of money but it was enough to cover the purchase of a team of horses and a wagon. From earlier conversations the person I was married to had warmed up to the idea of a horseback ride adventure all the way to Arizona. The plan eventually evolved into buying a team and building a wagon to shelter the girls and us. In April of that year we headed west. By the time we left we had acquired a few other horses for backup and selling along the way. Although we were traveling at only four miles per hour I was heading back to Arizona and in better spirits than I had been in years.

The job of driving the team was mine. Rocky followed along at the back of the wagon or was ridden. A full and detailed account of the next eighteen months is my first book, 'Buffalo Chips and Co.'

Rocky walked alongside the wagon the two hundred fifty miles from Carlton to Stanton, Texas with us. When extra horsepower was needed to

Rocky hobbled and grazing in the deep grass in front of our wagon near Brownwood, Texas, 1983

pull the wagon, Rocky pulled the wagon tongue via a rope dallied to the saddle horn. He was seriously injured while we were in Stanton, Texas and would not rejoin our wagon train until we arrived in Sun City, Arizona. Rocky cut his rear leg badly resulting in an infected tendon sheath and required not only the expertise of a veterinarian but a six-month layup. We were fortunate to have a local man by the name of Tommy Miracle offer to keep him until he was better. His only request was that we would take one of his young horses along with us to round off her education. The swap was made and I was comfortable with Rocky being in Tommy's care. As Rocky limped into Tommy's horse trailer I wasn't certain that I would ever see him again. I didn't know it would be a year before we could come back from Arizona to get him.

We arrived in Arizona in September. After wintering over in Chino Valley and Skull Valley we headed south to Sun City where another relative of my spouse lived. There we met a man that was planning a trip back to the same area of Texas that Rocky was in. Arrangements were made so that we could go along, taking Tommy's mare back to him to swap for Rocky.

It felt so good to see my horse again. Tommy had gone above and beyond the call of duty to help his leg heal. He had required another visit to the vet and was now completely sound again. Rocky now wore another scar on his back fetlock that he would carry the rest of his life.

After arriving back with Rocky we pointed the wagon north to escape the heat of the desert. Our destination again was Prescott. We stopped in Black Canyon City for a week to let the horses enjoy the green grass growing along the Agua Fria river on the west side of town. They stood in the cool water under the monstrous cottonwood trees and grazed the grass along the banks. It was horsey heaven. We made it up to Prescott in time for the Fourth of July and camped out at an old roping arena just off of Willow Creek road. After a few weeks we drove out to Coyote Springs and found a house to rent with acreage for our small group of horses. This property was known as Turtle Rock Ranch.

With much encouragement from me my spouse found work at a window factory in Prescott Valley. A friend of ours loaned us an old car to use until we could get our own. I had a small glimmer of hope that now we could live like other people but it was not to be. The job lasted two weeks. He had quit again. The excuse this time was that people there didn't like him. I had news for him. I didn't like him either, but he was my husband and I was raised to believe marriage was supposed to last till death do you part.

Within a few months of our arrival in Coyote Springs, the family I had just spent eighteen months walking away from moved back to Arizona. It was just a matter of weeks before we were once again living with them. I had just given birth to our third child at the house in Coyote Springs. Two days later an old mattress on the concrete floor in my in laws garage in Glendale was my new home. We could have had one of the spare bedrooms in the house but a brother and his wife and kids already occupied it. You would have thought I should have come down with a case of postpartum depression but I remained optimistic. Angry, yes, but still my hope for a happy life would not die. I went back to college during the day, and took a night job at a local drugstore chain. It was apparent that if I wanted to escape this family circus and have a place of my own to raise my children, I would have to be the one to make it happen.

Our few remaining horses now stayed on the outskirts of Sun City with an uncle. I drove out daily to care for them. My father in law's rented home came with an acre of horse property where he kept his own menagerie of livestock. Two more of his horses died before long, the victims of colic and bad hay. I was relieved that ours could be kept elsewhere. I didn't mind the drive out to tend to them. With my job I could buy good quality hay to feed them. They had a large area they shared on the east bank of the Agua Fria riverbed.

As soon as my small paychecks started coming I rented a tiny house near 75th Avenue and Grand Ave. It was a farming area but the property had no place for horses. Still it got us out from under the parent's roof. I was working from 11pm at night to 7:30 in the morning to make my paycheck but I was willing to do what it took to have my own place. The people we rented from had an old singlewide trailer for sale and with my steady job I was able to get a small loan to buy it within a few months. We had it delivered to a property not far from the uncles place where our horses were. My father in law had recently purchased the bare desert land consisting of two and a half acres.

Other than my spouse's uncle and his wife which I liked a lot, we had no neighbors for miles. It was a barren and desolate. Half of the property was in the river bottom. The other half where the trailer was parked was forty feet up the embankment. There was no well. There was no water. There was no electricity. There was no plumbing or septic. I had just bought a trailer that sat in the desert in the middle of nowhere without any utilities or hope of ever getting any, but I was literally a happy camper. I finally owned my own home and no longer lived with my in-laws.

After living in a horse drawn wagon for a year and a half I couldn't imagine that anything could possibly be worse. My daughters had their own bedroom. Rocky was contentedly swishing flies in the shade of a Palo Verde tree in the river bottom. All I had to do was make the one hundred twenty seven-dollar a month payment and this paradise could be ours to keep. I was living the American dream.

Oh yes, and I had to haul water. Water for the horses, water for washing dishes and water to drink and bathe. I was up to the task. We acquired six fifty five-gallon open top drums to transport the water. I bought an old pickup with my good credit and made payments on it too. My income covered the cost of groceries for our horses and us. Before long I had developed an at home business where I could be with my children, take care of Rocky and still bring in enough income to cover all our humble needs.

The desert surrounding us consisted of gravel and creosote bushes with a few ironwood and Palo Verde trees scattered throughout. Saguaro cacti and all their prickly relatives also shared the landscape. Coyotes could be heard howling at night and I was ever on the lookout for rattlesnakes. The most dangerous threat to my family's existence however was my spouse. Instead of mellowing as the years went by he became more sullen, violent and cruel. His apex of improvement to our new home was to hook up a small 12 volt TV to a wire that stretched out the screen less window to the trucks battery. He would spend his waking hours watching reruns of Andy Griffith and MASH. He took a job once at a door factory and was fired the next day. As far as I know that was the last job he ever had.

We lived in the desert in the metal-sided trailer for three years. It wasn't all bad. I could saddle Rocky and he and I explored the mile wide Agua Fria riverbed for miles up and downstream. There were miles and miles of jeep trails and paths meandering through the sparse brush to investigate. The desert in the springtime was carpeted with new grass and flowers. The weather was usually mild with soft breezes that brought the aroma of desert blossoms.

During the winters there was no better place to be to ride out the cold. This was apparent by the thousands of snowbirds from the northern states that flocked into the desert during the winter. These same people were an excellent market for my hand made and hand painted pottery that I created at home.

Sometimes in the winter the Bradshaw Mountains to the north of us would be dusted with snow. It could get cold but it was nothing compared to the icy blasts of the northern hemispheres. We had no heat inside the trailer except for the propane-stove burners to take off the early morning chill. I would take the worst of winter over a typical summer day any time.

For the span of three months the Sonoran desert summers baked us inside that metal trailer. The horses found shade from the thin cover of mesquite and ironwood trees. I hauled water from the corner store three miles to the south of us to keep their tank full. More often than not in the summer the man of the house would offer to take the truck and get water from his parent's place in Glendale fourteen miles away. He would leave around eight in the morning and return just before dark, spending the day in the air-conditioned comfort of his parent's house. I didn't really mind. It cut my suffering by half when he was gone. I only had to deal with the heat.

The trailer had few screens left on its windows. After opening all them as far as they could go I would soak sheets, pillow cases and towels in the horse trough and clothespin them to the rods over the windows. If there were any breeze at all it would cool the inside down to around a hundred degrees. If there were little or no wind I would fill a spray bottle and spritz the air inside like a mobile swamp cooler to help bring the temperature down. I kept a wet washcloth in a bowl to cool the children down.

The children also had a small plastic pool under a small Palo Verde tree behind the trailer to cool off in. At night it usually cooled off enough to sleep but it was common to wake up in the middle of the night with pools of sweat accumulating in your eyes. Sleeping outside would have been okay if we didn't have to sleep in the dirt. My fear of snakes kept me inside. We once found and killed two rattlesnakes in a matter of minutes. One rattler had crawled under the plastic pool and his friend had slithered under the steps at the front door.

Dust storms were always a special treat. They occurred in the hot afternoons during monsoon season. I always welcomed the breeze but the dirt that came with them must have originated in the dust bowl days. The heat kept me from closing the windows and when the storm hit the inside of the trailer was powdered with dirt. I had to sweep the house with a broom because there was no vacuum or electric to use a vacuum cleaner even if I had one. The counters would need wiped down, the bathtub, the linoleum floors and the toilet. I could have started a garden with the fresh blown dirt that accumulated. Just because we were poor didn't mean we were dirty. It just took a lot more effort to keep up.

I heated dishwater on the stove in a pan. We hooked up a five-gallon propane tank to the range so I could at least cook. Our refrigerator was the same one we used on the wagon trip. A simple Styrofoam box that held a block of ice and a gallon of milk. The last year we lived there a woman I met in my college art class, Maggie Bryce, had pity on us and loaned us a Servel propane refrigerator.

As I stated before we had no plumbing. The waste from the toilet plopped on the ground underneath the trailer. It did so after I walked out to the horse trough and carried buckets of water into the house to flush it once a day. I thought perhaps if my husband wasn't busy he might take over that chore and asked him once to do so. He growled that he'd do it but the day came and went. Then the next and the next and the one after that. After a week went by I broke down and did it myself. It was starting to reach the top of the bowl and I knew that if it ran over the top I would get to clean that mess up too.

We didn't get many visitors out at our home in the desert. I suppose we lived a little too rough for even my spouse's family. They seldom showed up. The order still stood that I wouldn't have friends or my family come to visit either. I was actually relieved. I was ashamed to have anyone see how we lived.

One day my husband's younger brother came out to our desert estate to go horseback riding. Rocky was to be his mount for the ride and I wasn't happy about it. This younger psychopath sibling of my spouse had shot and killed my dog a few years back for no other reason than target practice. I did not wish him well. He and his role model of a big brother saddled up and rode down into the riverbed. That's where Rocky took vengeance for me. Bless his heart. Rocky bucked the lying, stealing, dog murdering lazy bastard off. I made a vow right then and there to keep ol' Rocky till the day he died.

I really loved that horse.

One summer my friend Maggie from my art class at college to pity on me and invited us to spend a couple of months with her at her ranch in

Rocky, Ranger and Peter Pony at Deerhead Ranch.

the White Mountains. I jumped at the chance to escape the desert heat. Maggie told us we could bring the horses, kids and a tent to sleep in. She'd provide the food. Such a deal! Sleeping in a tent for two months in the mountains would be a lot more comfortable than sweating it out on the desert floor. We borrowed the old decrepit four-horse open-top stock trailer from my father-in-law, hooked up to the pickup and headed east for eight hours. Maggie's ranch was as beautiful as she said it would be. She met us at the highway where the jeep trail led off the pavement to the ranch. It would be a two-hour horseback ride in. We parked the truck and trailer between the pine trees near a catch pen and unloaded our horses. We had our five animals comfortably crammed into the four-horse trailer. Two ponies shared a space. Rocky and another horse and a mule used up the other three spots. It had been a long drive and they were all happy to get out.

After saddling up Rocky and the other horse my spouse and I led the ponies and mule down the trail. Maggie let the children ride in her four-wheel drive Blazer. The ranch was only six miles away but even in a vehicle the trip would take an hour. The road was rough and winding and left no room for error. Along the way Maggie pointed out where a forest service truck had tumbled off the slick road into a steep ravine, and then showed us the tree that had caught her husband's truck when it slipped over the edge. Some of the hairpin turns had been washed away by the heavy summer rains and the road that was left was barely wide enough for Maggie's Blazer to cross.

We arrived just before dark and settled the horses into their temporary quarters. They would have run of the ranch and could graze for the next eight weeks on the high mountain grasses. We hastily pitched our little tent near a giant alligator-bark cedar tree. Maggie cooked up a quick dinner and we all slept comfortably in the cool mountain air.

The Deerhead Ranch was located an hour north of Morenci off the two-lane road known at Arizona State Route 666. The Devil's Highway. It's also known at the Coronado Trail Scenic Byway. It has more twists and turns than a plate of spaghetti. A great number of them are posted at just ten miles per hour. Right before Grey's Peak a jeep trail on the left leads off towards the ranch. After heading north and climbing the twenty miles or so from Morenci the road to the ranch wiggled west towards Eagle Creek. Maggie and her husband had recently bought the remote ranch and were in the process of building a house. Thus far they had built a spacious two-hole outhouse and had piped the Deerhead spring to their campsite. The spring water flowed into an old whiskey barrel day and night without ceasing. If we needed water for drinking, cooking or bathing we had but to walk to the barrel. This place had running water. Ah, I thought, the conveniences of modern living!

Maggie stayed in a small fourteen-foot travel trailer parked in the shade of some large oak trees. Meals could be prepared inside and brought out to the folks seated on the many chairs and tree stumps scattered around the campfire ring. Maggie also had a screened in tent set up under the trees between the dry Deerhead creek bed and our tent. She used this area to do her artwork. An easel was set up inside where she could work on her oil paintings. Maggie invited me to paint with her whenever I liked. Our summer was spent riding around the ranch, doing our daily chores and painting.

One of our first outings was a horseback trip across to an adjoining ranch. The trail took us back out onto the road that we had rode in on and then about a third of the way back up the mountain we headed south. That's where we turned to follow an old cow trail that led across some caprock to the steep trail leading down to the neighboring ranch's headquarters.

I reined Rocky off the main trail and across a wide area that was naturally flat due to the exposed rock. As we started walking across the largest flat rock on the top of the rise I looked down and spied a carving in the rock. I brought Rocky to a stop and gazed down at an odd sight. Here on the top of this knoll was a large carved symbol and a date. Being that we were so far out in the boonies as anyone could possibly be, this ornately carved rock seemed very out of place. It obviously had taken several hours to complete. It was not something that a passing cowboy would take the time to do. The marker was large, about twenty-four inches or more across in both directions. The main symbol was a large X or a cross. The date, if correct, made no sense as it was centuries old. I remember thinking 'the pilgrims haven't even landed on Plymouth Rock yet!'

Calling the other riders over they too gave it a puzzled look. None of us comprehended at the time what it could possibly mean. Years later it occurred to me that it was a good possibility I had ridden Rocky across a marker that had been carved permanently in that rock by the Coronado expedition to mark their trail. There was a reason the pavement a few miles to the east had been named the Coronado Trail. It's been many years since that day but I'm sure I could find it again with little effort. It's on my bucket list.

Half way into our stay the rainy monsoon season started up. Each morning the nights cool air would slowly give way to the ever rising sun in the east. By midday it was warm and we could watch small clouds begin to form over the mountaintops on all sides of the ranch. As the afternoon progressed the remote canyons and valleys to the south darkened with thunderstorms. Lightning would split the sky against the dark clouds and my girls would count the seconds until we heard the distant thunder. Five, six, seven, eight and then, boom! Sometimes it rained on the ranch and sometimes it seemed the rain stopped right at the gate.

One evening after finishing our supper we retreated to our beds in the tent under a light sprinkle of much needed rain. The afternoon monsoon had finally made its way to the Deerhead Ranch. We could hear the rain softly pecking on the roof of the tent as we dozed off to sleep. The temperature had dropped considerably and the inside of the tent was almost comfortable. In less than an hour our sleep was interrupted by the crack of thunder that accompanied a white flash that had just lit up the entire ranch. The rain that was pounding on the roof of the tent immediately grew heavier. Another flash and lightning struck again. After witnessing the deadly consequences of a lightning strike many years before my concern was for our horses out on the hillside. The lightning cracked again.

There were some large alligator cedars near us that I feared might take a hit. When Mother Nature unleashes her fury a canvas tent is not much of a refuge. Still, the rain bounced off the roof and sides and we were relatively dry. The tent had been pitched above a dry narrow creek bed that was no more than ten feet wide. Upstream about three hundred yards was the Deerhead Spring. Beyond that the dry creek went nearly vertical up into a wide crevice that snaked its way up into the mountains north of us. It had been dry all summer and because the tent was at least eight feet higher than the closest bank we gave it no thought.

The lightning and thunder had just started warming up. Sleep was impossible for any length of time. It was as if the mountains on either side of us were throwing spikes of lightning back and forth at each other in some kind of weird battle and it went on for hours. We were in no-man's land between the two. Finally the battle slowed and exhausted we fell back asleep. I could hear the creek below us running now but the worst was over. I slowly floated off to sleep. Floating, floating into oblivion. Then I snapped back to reality.

We were floating. The creek had risen over eight feet and had spread out on both sides of its banks. Because the tent had a sewn in water-proof bottom the swollen edge of the creek was passing under it. Only the tent stakes held it in place. Our roughing it on the hard ground had literally evolved into a comfortable waterbed. I woke the children and stood up to unzip the entrance. Our movement had caused the water to enter in at the doorway in a rush and in seconds all our bedding was soaked. I grabbed my youngest and with my two daughters in tow slipped through the opening into six inches of cold muddy water rushing around my bare feet and legs. Their dad followed behind after zipping up the doorway. The rain was beating down harder than before. In total darkness we rushed uphill towards Maggie's camp trailer and beat on the door. She was already awake from the night's storm and quickly let her soaked guests in. I put the children on the tiny sofa and covered them with some bedding. Maggie hastily found some extra blankets and I collapsed on a flat spot on the floor big enough to stretch out on and fell asleep wondering if the tent would be gone in the morning.

At daylight I stumbled out to inspect the damage and look for my missing boots. The swollen creek had made its mark. Maggie's little tent studio got the brunt of it because it was closest to the creek. The flood-water had disappeared downstream along with some of her paintings, my pottery, brushes, easels and more. Both tents were flattened. Inside ours all the blankets were wet and covered with mud. The pillows were soaked through and filthy.

After accessing our tent home and retrieving my wet boots I climbed to higher ground to find Rocky and the other horses. I could see them grazing on the far side of the pasture. After doing a quick nose count and finding one of the ponies that was hidden from view behind a bigger horse, I sighed, thankful the storm didn't do any more damage than it did.

My daughters spent the day looking downstream for their lost herd of 'My Little Ponies' and were able to rescue a couple that had been caught in the roots of brush along the flood's path. The remaining herd had been lost forever and may have even made it all the way to the Salt River. Maggie found one of her paintings a mile downstream. My unfired pottery had returned back to the earth from whence it came. After pulling out our bedding I hand washed it and spread it out to dry. The sun came out to help dry things off and we shook out the tent and set it back up where only a flood of Biblical proportions could touch it.

Prior to our arrival at the ranch, my husband had been hired to break the mule we brought with us. He intended to complete this task while we stayed the eight weeks at the Deerhead Ranch. Other than being halter broke it had no training whatsoever. Instead of working with the mule the procrastinating trainer chose rather to dig around for relics in the nearby abandoned Indian campsite for nearly six weeks. A phone call from the owner finally prompted him to get off his ass onto the one he was supposed to be training. The owner said he would be visiting in a few days to see how well his mule was doing.

The next morning the last minute mule training began. The plan was to get a saddle on the critter and then ride him. For a mule, he was gentle enough, but if rushed during the training you could expect the worse. No one in his right mind would attempt such a thing. Not with a mule and I wanted no part of it. Besides, I wasn't the one hired to do the job. I had three little children to care for and getting hurt or breaking a limb hours away from the closest town was not high on my list of things to do. However it was not a big surprise when I was ordered to get my horse and become a part of another person's train wreck.

After saddling up Rocky I returned to find the mule lying on the ground with all four feet tied up. The saddle was on and secured and I was handed the lead rope. When loosed the mule stood up and I led him around. He didn't do a darn thing. I had expected the bomb to go off but it didn't. I was content to lead him all around the ranch, letting him get used to all the new stuff now tied to his back. Asking any more of him on his first day of school would be a bad idea. But before long Mr. Bad Idea decided he would climb aboard and I could continue leading the mule. In the event the mule blew up I had already decided to turn the teacher loose with his student and let them work it out. There wasn't room in my saddle for a bucking mule with its rider and I had no desire to risk injury to my horse or myself because of someone else's bad choices.

My friend Maggie knew what the situation was and grabbed her camera to record the string of Kodak moments that were certainly about to happen. After the rider settled himself upon the mule I was ordered to step out. Three steps later the mule began to kick, the camera began to click, then the mule went airborne with his new found freedom and Maggie and I watched the bucking beast take out across the pasture with its trainer. Because of the recent rains the ground was soft and with each jump the mule sunk nearly to his knees in the mud. We could hear sucking popping sounds as the earth reluctantly released the long-eared hybrid with every leap. The rider broke the clear pristine air with a string of loud profanity that faded away as they bucked and farted their way across the pasture and into the sunset.

Ponying the unbroken mule with Rocky.

It was a good thing my friend was there when the pair returned. I knew I was in deep trouble for running away from the circus. After a string of profanities hurled my way, the rider jerked the mule around and rode away. They traveled all over the ranch that day but never in a straight line. I was grateful that evening when the mule trainer returned too exhausted to carry out any of his previous threats.

The last weekend we stayed at the Deerhead Ranch was also the weekend of the Greenlee County annual Cattle Growers Picnic and Barbecue. We had been invited and all of us tumbled into Maggie's Blazer to make the two hour drive over the mountain to Eagle Creek. For the potluck we made a big platter of homemade enchiladas. Most of the meat in the small freezer had been used up during the summer. Maggie pulled out the last package for the event. It was the last of one of her kids. Goat kids. We said nothing as we all sat down to dinner and watched the cattlemen of Greenlee County wolf down those goat enchiladas two and three at a time.

The picnic was held right on the banks of Eagle Creek. I do believe that area is the most beautiful place in all of Arizona. The cowboy artist Tim Cox lived there and the scenery in his paintings reflect those surroundings.

Maggie introduced us to Stella Hughes, an author and another of her friends, who in turn invited us over to Tim Cox's place on Eagle Creek. Tim showed us his most recent works and the ones in progress. I had brought some of the pottery I had made in hopes of selling some pieces at the picnic and showed some of them to Tim. He bought a vase to keep his brushes in. I was honored. Tim then brought out his young mare to their front lawn and put her through the string of tricks he had taught her. The last one was for her to lay down right there on the trimmed grass. The grass must have felt really good as she was content to lie there for quite awhile.

My children had the entire day to play with other youngsters along the creek. The tall cottonwoods and downed timber made for great fort building and hideouts. A rope swing dangled invitingly from one of the tall trees. One of the rancher's boys had brought his pony and all the

Moving cows with Rocky at the Deerhead Ranch

children took turns riding him around and through the shallow waters of Eagle Creek. Finally the day ended and we said our good-byes. The children were all asleep before we reached the pavement of Highway 666 and turned south back towards the Deerhead.

The next morning I was awakened by the sound of galloping hooves and singing wire whizzing close to our tent. Rocky had caught the lowest wire of a line of field fence between his hoof and front shoe and decided to take it to the far end of the ranch. The heavy round wire must have been at least thirty feet long. As he panicked and ran down the road it startled the whole herd and we encountered a stampede running and circling with him as he tried to outrun the monster. I grabbed a fence tool and caught up with Rocky near the front gate. He stood snorting and shaking. Gingerly I approached the wire and carefully cut it off a few feet behind him. Then I got the halter on Rocky that had been brought down by one of my daughters. I stroked Rocky's neck and calmed him, then reached down and cut the wire close to the shoe. The piece still stuck would have to be removed by taking the shoe off. There were no injuries. The shoe was reset and we spent the day preparing for the long drive home.

At daybreak the next day we saddled our stock and started the climb out to the highway six miles away. I was not looking forward to spending the remainder of the summer on the banks of the Agua Fria in a metal sided trailer house.

Back in the desert my marriage continued to dissolve. My husband was still unemployed after fourteen years and my hope for a normal life seemed futile. Rocky was my refuge. With my children in school and the husband gone to spend the day with his parents I could saddle up Rocky and fade away into the desert. These times gave me a place to reflect on my life and contemplate my future. Things looked pretty dismal. In the middle of nowhere I would sometimes cry as I rode along, Rocky's mane catching my tears. Rocky was always a good listener and I could share my troubles with him. The wild scenery we rode through always helped uplift my spirits.

One morning I pointed Rocky east instead of west across the Agua Fria and rode several miles towards 83rd Ave. I had been feeling abused, isolated, and powerless. The outside of my horse would do the inside of this cowgirl some good. As I rode along I thought of all my decisions both good and bad, and the consequences of each. I tried to imagine a better future for my children and myself but all I could see was a dead end. At least it would be for me. My husband had become more and more violent and I knew without a doubt that if I did not find a way out soon he would probably bury me in the desert and no one would find my remains. Maybe I could survive another two years at best. Feeling hopeless I knew something needed to change. I was afraid and I prayed for deliverance.

Riding along on Rocky helped me clear my mind and focus on other things. I could see 83rd Ave in the distance now and knew I didn't want to cross it. Beyond it housing developments merged with others to form a concrete, asphalt, and stucco city for a million people. I reined Rocky to the south and we went through fields of bulldozed orange groves that the desert was desperately trying to reclaim before the developers arrived. Just south of Union Hills Drive a new subdivision had popped out of a former citrus orchard. It sat alone in the center of a larger area that had been stripped of its former lemon and orange groves. Instead of riding around to the south or retracing my steps to the north I chose to ride quietly through the middle of it. From the empty field I was in I could see that one of the paved streets was much wider than the others and I chose it for my shortcut back to the west.

Rocky stepped out of the desert onto the black asphalt that led between the manicured homes. As we clip clopped along this neighborhood street I looked at the pretty homes so neatly crammed together with their perfectly landscaped yards. Perplexed I wondered how people could afford homes such as these with electricity and running water and toilets that flushed themselves. The street was deserted. Not one person noticed our passing. Only one lonely car came from the west and drove by. I waved politely to the driver but got no response. The road curved slightly to the south and I could see the desert beyond beckoning us away from civilization.

To my left stood another house in the long line of homes we had just passed. There was nothing visible or remarkable that made this home stand out from the rest. It blended in so well with the others I gave it no notice at all. Had I known the significance of it at that time I believe I would have stopped to take a closer look. It was the home belonging to the twin brother of the man I would be marrying six years into the future. Even in my darkness lights would flicker. I just couldn't see them.

It was a long and nasty divorce. Marriage only takes a few minutes. Divorce can last years as did mine. My estranged husband feared child support and the laws that went along with it more than anything else. He felt it would be best for him to have custody of our three so that I could continue being the breadwinner that I had been for so many years. That way he could avoid employment and continue his lifestyle. I wasn't concerned about receiving any child support from him. He hadn't provided for his family for most of the last fourteen years and I knew nothing would change. I was content to have him gone. That was payment enough. I could provide for my children just like I always did.

Two months after dropping him off at his parents to live for the next few decades, my trailer in the desert burned to the ground. This happened after my soon to be divorced husband came out with his dad's truck and removed everything that he wanted while I was gone. With my home reduced to ashes and twisted metal, my children and I stayed with a my artist friend, Marilyn Sixel, until I could scrape up enough to get a new place to live. Rocky and the other horses stayed there, in the desert, and I drove out twice a day to feed and water them. It was an uncomfortable situation. I didn't want to leave Rocky there but I had nowhere else to take him.

My estranged husband was fine with me continuing to provide and care for our daughters' ponies and other horses. He still was unemployed and I think his dad was not too keen on adopting our small herd. I made it known that I intended to continue feeding and caring for all of them, and I would be moving all of them as soon as I could. My ex at that point informed me that all the horses belonged to him, including Rocky. My heart sank. Desperation flowed over me. I couldn't leave Rocky there any longer. I had no place to take him and no trailer to get him there if I did.

Divorce papers had been filed, and I naively thought, fine, we'll let the judge decide who gets the horses. My attorney however told me that because I purchased Rocky prior to the marriage, he was considered 'sole and separate property'. I could legally retrieve my horse. A relative of my ex came to my rescue. His cousin Susan lived close by and gave me permission to use her old horse trailer. She even came with me for support in the event my ex showed up and started trouble. Another of my friends, Anita, allowed me to put a tiny temporary pen up at her home for Rocky until I could move him. Within a few weeks I had returned back to the Turtle Rock Ranch in Coyote Springs and settled in, taking Rocky with me.

I felt sick knowing the other ponies and horses would be left in my ex's care. He would not take any better care of them than he did his family. Because I didn't want a battle I resigned myself to their fate and told myself I had to wait and play according to the rules until the judge decided. Two of them died of thirst and starvation before we ever got to court. When the second one died the Arizona Livestock Board got involved, seized the survivors, then later returned them with the stipulation they would be taken to my father-in-law's home. In court my ex lied and said the remaining ponies and horses had been sold. I wasn't surprised. A good arsonist is also a good liar.

To this day I do not understand how the Livestock Board did not charge the person responsible with animal cruelty and neglect. Ranger and another pony died of thirst and starvation. Because I had moved nearly a hundred miles away I had no idea of their condition and naïvely waited for a court date to ask permission to go get my own ponies. My ex had no interest in taking care of them. He only wanted to make sure I didn't get them and he knew that by hurting them it hurt me. It was his primary motivation. Years later I was able to track down the pony that accompanied us on the wagon trip, Peter Pony, and got

Ranger starving to death with no water in the tank to drink.

him back. He died of old age, fat and sassy. He's the one in the photo behind Ranger.

Meanwhile back at the Turtle Rock Ranch I was doing a fine job of rebuilding my life. I had developed an at home business to provide for my children, my home had a toilet that flushed, and Rocky had ten acres to himself. Being my own boss I could work as needed and sometimes slip off in the middle of the day on Rocky while the children were in school.

PART THREE

A FRESH START!

During the next four years that my children and I lived at the Turtle Rock my life renewed. I was free! By the time the 'Decree of Disillusionment' was signed I had proven to myself I was fully capable of earning a decent living for my family and could provide for their needs and a few of their wants without any help from anyone. As predicted the child support from my ex never appeared. The judge let him off easy with a $50 a month payment for all three children combined and he never paid a dime. It was a joke. You may ask yourself "But what about the child support laws?" Those are for women on welfare, which I was not. Common sense told me not to waste thousands on an attorney to gain fifty dollars. It was not an issue to me. I was having too much fun enjoying a simple life. The homes in Coyote Springs were few and far between and I liked the wide-open spaces. To the west lay Chino Valley and the hills and prairies Rocky and I explored years before. Mingus and Woodchute Mountain were just a few miles east of the Turtle Rock. My beloved Verde River was about twenty miles to the north. Very few fence lines separated Rocky and me from the wilderness I loved so much. Although he was close to twenty years of age Rocky hadn't slowed down a bit.

Not long after moving back a neighbor stopped in to say hello. Her name was Rebecca and we became close friends. She too had horses and loved to ride. Because I needed help with my home business I hired her to help me as she could. It wasn't uncommon for us to be in the middle of a project, feel the spring breeze and then look at each other as if to say "What are we doing here? Let's saddle up!" Within minutes we would meet up and ride for a few hours. The work would be waiting when we got back. I could always put in a few hours after the children were in bed if need be. There was plenty to do.

The foothills of Mingus Mountain were only a half-hour ride away.

At the north end the narrow gauge railroad bed still trailed its way around the mountain to Jerome. It was driveable with a vehicle but I seldom saw anyone on it, as it was not maintained. Uncle Dale had told me he had ridden on the original narrow gauge train when his family first arrived in the area. They boarded in Chino Valley and rode it to the Verde Valley. He was just a boy then. Dale said the grass everywhere was as tall as your stirrups. There was no erosion or washes anywhere to be seen. All the rivers were so choked with vegetation you could hardly ride your horse up to the water's edge.

The mine in Jerome was in full production back then and Dale told me about a piece of machinery he watched being pulled up the winding streets by mules. He said there was twenty teams hitched to pull the heavy machine. He watched them snake their way up and around the hairpin corners of Jerome on their way to the mine. The mules were on a jerkline and the driver could not see his mules at the lead because they were so far away and hidden by the curves in the road. On the tight corners the mules were trained to jump the chain that separated them so they would not fall down as they turned a corner. It was quite a sight! It took several hours for them to negotiate the narrow winding road that went through the main part of town.

Taken near the railroad cliff overhang.

On the Chino Valley side of the narrow gauge just as it starts into the foothills Rocky and I found a cliff overhang that overlooked the former railroad bed. It was just below the top off a hill to the west of Matthews Peak. Under the canopy of rock the names and dates of some of the railroad workers were carved into the rock. The previous photo shows the view from this place with Big Chino Valley in the distance.

With nothing else to do, my ex was still trying to figure out how his cash cow, (me) had escaped his grip. During, and even after the divorce, he continually dragged me back into court for custody issues. Although each time he lost ground he would come back for more. I found the whole thing preposterous and a huge waste of my time and money. He never gained an inch. In his anger he did whatever he could to cause me pain or grief. I was hoping he would move on when he took up with his brothers ex girlfriend Mary. Instead they conspired along with his Mary's uncle to hit me where it would really hurt.

My weekends were usually spent out of town at an arts and crafts fair somewhere in the southwest. I traveled a lot to sell my art and pottery. It was how I made my living. I did not like having to be away from home but there was no other option. I had children, rent and bills to pay. On my way home from a show in Nevada I stopped to call my parents. They told me they had driven out to check on my place and wanted to know if I had moved Rocky as they couldn't see him out in the pasture. Oh, and they said the front fence had been cut next to the gate. My heart stopped. Rocky had been stolen!

I arrived home just before midnight and confirmed their observation. Rocky was gone. My gate was still locked, but I could see that the fence next to it had been cut through. I called the sheriff and in less than an hour an officer arrived. She made an incident report and left. A stolen horse wasn't a big deal for the sheriff's department.

It was a very big deal for me though. I knew in my gut who had stolen him. I just prayed they hadn't hauled him to an auction and Rocky was being cut up on the floor of a slaughterhouse in Mexico.

I didn't sleep much that night. At first light I went out to look for the tracks left by the horse thief. I could see where a vehicle had pulled into the softer dirt at the side of the road. This confused me. The tires of the thief's truck had really good tread, like snow tires. No one in my ex's extended family ever had anything but nearly bald worn out tires on anything they owned. The truck that hauled Rocky away had four new tires. I was perplexed. The trailer was the same way. I took photos of the tracks and started my search. I knew the girlfriend had an uncle that lived in Camp Verde and he had horses. My daughters had told this information to me. Perhaps they had taken Rocky there. I contacted the Arizona Livestock Board as soon as they opened and made a report. I grabbed a recent photo of Rocky and plastered flyers everywhere, sent some to all the in-state auction yards and called everyone I could to put the word out. By the middle of the week I had found out the name of Mary's uncle.

I contacted the Arizona Livestock Board inspector for the Verde Valley and asked him to go look over the uncle's place to see if my horse was there. A few hours later he called back and said he didn't see any horses there but there was a blind spot over a rise you couldn't see from the road. I wasn't satisfied so on Saturday I loaded my kids and drove to Camp Verde. My oldest daughter had been to the property before and gave me directions to the uncle's place. It did not match the address the inspector gave me. As we drove down the dirt road she pointed out his trailer and there, standing with two other horses was Rocky. My heart leapt! I drove on around the corner and went straight back to a sheriff's station we had passed coming in. I left the kids in the truck, went in and explained the situation. I showed the sheriff the incident report and asked if an officer would go with me to get my horse. Rocky was only two miles away and I wanted him back in my possession immediately.

As it turned out the officer knew this man but not as the criminal he apparently was. When we got to the property the officer left me in the car and went to the door. In a few moments he came back and told me "You can go get your horse right now, but you will not press charges. That's the deal." Getting Rocky back in my possession was my utmost priority. I agreed but it felt wrong. The sheriff handed me the halter and lead rope that had also been stolen out of my barn and I opened the gate into the corral. I led Rocky out into the driveway and asked the officer for a leg up. Before he got back in his squad car he told me to ride Rocky to his house, the one he pointed out close to the sheriff's station. I could leave Rocky there until I returned with my trailer. The officer preceded me out the long driveway. When he turned onto the street the uncle came running out of his house to stop me. I pushed Rocky into a trot and rode him out onto the highway without looking back. Tears were running down my cheeks as I rode Rocky out onto the main road into Camp Verde with only a halter and lead rope to guide him.

It was about two miles back to the officer's home. Upon arrival I led Rocky to the corral out back and told the officer I would be coming back immediately to pick Rocky up. I did not feel comfortable leaving Rocky with an acquaintance of a horse thief. He once again made the statement that I would not press charges. I had my horse back and that was enough.

After I had Rocky loaded into a trailer and headed home I started to contemplate the officers comment. When is a thief not a thief? Why couldn't I press charges? I had lost time away from my work, suffered much anguish and spent a lot of money on gasoline and flyers. It didn't seem right. If Mary and her uncle had stolen my car, and then I got it back, would I be told not to press charges? Why didn't they get arrested? Perhaps I'll never know the reason. As we headed for home it occurred to me that the officer had not told me I couldn't file for damages. A smile came across my face. The first one that had been there all week. I filed. And won. Thank you Judge Wagner.

I could only imagine the rage my ex husband felt with his foiled theft. My fear for Rocky being stolen again or shot and killed caused me to find a safer place to keep him. Once again, my longtime friend Ann Heckethorn came to the rescue. She had an empty corral to keep him for me under her watchful eye. I bought several bags of alfalfa horse pellets for his feed and dropped them off at Ann's. I would have preferred to keep Rocky at home, but my schedule for the next few weekends would put me out of town and Rocky at risk. Ann's place was about eight miles away from mine and I didn't think my ex had the testicular fortitude to try anything there.

About three weeks later Ann found me at a local show and walked over to my booth. Her face looked concerned. "You need to come look at Rocky. The vet just left. He's really sick and the vet said he didn't think he'd make it through the night." "What's wrong?" I asked. Rocky had seldom been sick. Ann said the vet wasn't sure, but that he thought his heart was enlarged and he was having trouble breathing. We left immediately.

As I pulled up to Rocky's corral I could see his distress. He was standing with his head down, coughing. Green slime dripped out of his nose. Ann and I looked with anguish at my poor old gelding. I told Ann, "I'm going to get the trailer and take him home to die." Rocky was visibly weak as he walked into the trailer. I feared he wouldn't make it home. Much to my relief he survived the trip and I backed him out of the trailer. He was still weak but lifted his head with recognition of his surroundings. I led him through the gate and with teary eyes hugged Rocky's neck, perhaps for the last time. Then took off his halter and turned him loose. He plodded off towards the far end of his ten acres. Twenty years was old for a horse. Maybe it was just his time to go.

It was almost dark by now. After fixing dinner for the children they played some games and then headed for bed. I worried that I would only see a brown lump lying still in the pasture the next morning.

I was up before the children, which was normal. The sun had not broke over Mingus Mountain yet but it was light enough to see. Putting on my boots I stepped out the back door. To the east I could see the majority of the pasture. There was nothing there except the yellowed Chino grass standing erect in the breezeless morning. I walked to the west side of the barn to get a view of the back of the pasture. There was no horse their either. I walked across the front entrance to his stall and heard a hearty nicker from inside the barn. Rocky was standing at his feeder impatiently waiting for his breakfast! He wasn't even close to checking out. He tossed his head and swatted his tail at a fly. With much joy I threw him a flake of hay and Rocky picked it up and dismantled it by tossing it up and down, scattering dried alfalfa leaves around his feeder.

This miracle recovery jogged my memory to an event that happened years ago. Rocky was in a two horse trailer being pulled along and bouncing over a bumpy road. In the feeder at the front of the trailer some horse pellets remained from the previous trip. Upon unloading Rocky at our destination he came out of the trailer coughing and spitting up green slime and horse pellets. He was choking. Rocky was choking at Ann's too. Green slime coming out his nose and mouth, coughing. Why didn't the vet catch this? If Rocky's heart was enlarged it was because he couldn't breathe. I called Ann and told her the good news. Rocky wasn't dead and I expected him to live a long time.

As my children were getting older and we could afford it I purchased another horse. Rocky would be happy to have a pasture pal and now that the girls ponies were dead or gone we started looking. A girlfriend in the Phoenix area was going through a divorce and she offered me an unbroken paint mare. Unlike my ex, hers didn't want anything to do with her horses.

The price was right and I brought her home. She had been handled since birth but not ridden and was just coming three.

This little paint mare had been in the same corral her whole life. It was time to expand her horizons so Rocky and I took her for a walk around her new neighborhood. She had never experienced the great outdoors, walking through rough rocky areas or having to watch for cactus. Like a kid raised up in the city she was accustomed to loud radios and roaring engines, but not jackrabbits bounding out from under the brush or being startled by quail flying in front of her face. Miles and miles in tow next to Rocky expanded her worldview and made her a better horse. My oldest daughter began riding her in the pasture with just a halter. She turned out to be a good solid family horse.

A spry 23-year-old Rocky ponies a young mare.

As Rocky grew older he started having problems with his teeth. Horse dentistry was not as available back then as it is now. I had a vet come out and use a float on Rocky but it didn't help much. One of his upper molars was missing and the opposing lower tooth was growing into the open space from the bottom. Rocky was starting to lose weight and he was spitting out small balls of partially chewed hay. I scheduled an appointment with the most expensive and best-equipped horse vet in the area and took Rocky in. We put Rocky in the stocks and the vet took a good look at the problem. It was decided that the easiest thing to do was knock Rocky out and crawl inside his mouth with bolt cutters to cut the offending tooth down to size. I brought my video camera to record the event.

After the vet gave Rocky a sedative shot to make him droopy, I led him into a padded room next door. Rocky stood swaying in the center of the room. The vet's assistant shoved Rocky towards the far wall. Then the vet gave him the anesthesia to drop him. Except Rocky didn't drop. He backed his butt into the corner, leaned up against the wall, propped all four legs and passed out standing up. No respectable ranch raised horse would lie down in the presence of his enemies or predators or anyone else for that matter. He felt no reason to do so now. During the years Rocky and I were partners if I approached him while he was laying down he would always quickly stand up. Rocky would never allow anyone to catch him laying down on the job. That would be too humbling an experience for him. Rocky would meet you eye to eye.

It took four of us to pry Rocky off the wall. He finally fell with a thud onto the padded floor. Two assistants pointed his nose towards the ceiling and opened his mouth. A huge three foot long bolt cutter was inserted into his massive open maw and the vet strained with all his might before a chunk of tooth popped loose. It wasn't enough though and he went back for seconds. Another vet came in to watch and was recruited to break off two more chunks. A total of four half inch long pieces of tooth were cut out of Rocky's mouth. I still have them. The float was then used to take off the sharp edges. The whole procedure lasted about twenty minutes. Rocky would finish his nap and I would take him home in a few hours. The little balls of hay went away and never returned.

One weekend a friend and I saddled up and rode the six miles down to a small convenience store on the backside of Prescott Valley. It was a warm summer day and the thought of a cold soda pop sounded real refreshing. This little store was the closest sign of civilization for the few people who lived in Coyote Springs. We bought our pops and walked our horses across the pavement to where a gentleman was selling ranch relics and bleached cow skulls at the side of the road. I saw him there often on weekends and never had the time to stop and chat.

I stood next to Rocky while we spoke, my right arm lazily stretched over the back of my saddle. In the blink of an eye Rocky flinched as if he had been stung. As I stepped back to see if I could figure out what had caused him to flinch. Without warning Rocky cow kicked me so hard it actually burned the jeans I was wearing as if a hot iron had tried to burn a hole clean through. Rocky struck me in the side of my leg just below my knee. I grabbed a hold of my saddle horn to keep standing up and catch my breath. The pain was indescribable. I held back the tears and felt myself retreat into shock. I couldn't drop my jeans to check the damage but I couldn't see any blood seeping through. My instinct was to return home so we did. I could barely climb back up on Rocky and I rode with my leg dangling on the off side the six miles back. When I dismounted my leg was useless and I only kept myself from falling by hanging onto my saddle horn as I dismounted.

At home I inspected where he hit me and the area had already turned black and blue and purple. By the next morning my leg from my foot up felt like it was on fire. My leg had turned purple spreading all the way from my foot nearly to the top of my hip. For some reason it never occurred to me to go to a doctor. As I look back now it was a miracle I didn't get a blood clot. I was two weeks getting back to using my leg. It hurt for months afterwards. The bone is dented to this day just below my knee. At twenty-three years of age Rocky was still capable of doing damage.

One of my friends was a caretaker for an elderly rancher in Granite Dells. One weekend she invited us to come out to the ranch and bring our horses. We met one of the rancher's sons when we arrived and he kindly offered to take us for a tour of his father's homestead, known as the Storm Ranch.

The Storm Ranch was situated in a forest of gigantic granite boulders that surrounded the Willow and Watson lakes. This was one place where a guide would be a necessity as the trails through the boulders wound their way around like a labyrinth.

As we rode along our guide told us about how his father, an old time cowboy, would race his horse across the face of the large granite boulders at breakneck speed to catch a cow. Sometimes the trails between the boulders were no wider than a horse's hoof. Other times they disappeared all together and your horse had to climb up and over the huge rock in the trail only to be met by another larger one to climb over and then you could slide down the far side to the bottom. This was extreme trail riding and I loved it. The cattle were kept in pastures along the east side of Watson Lake and as far away as Glassford Hill.

Watson Lake through Rocky's ever pricked ears.

Years ago I heard about a camp some outlaws had hidden deep in this maze of boulders. I could see why it would be hard to find anyone in there. Finally we broke through to an open area and found ourselves looking down upon Watson Lake. As we came down off the ridge I took a photo of the view over Rocky's ever-erect ears.

Our lives at the Turtle Rock Ranch had improved much over the years compared to what my family and I had already endured. Although we lived there for many years off the grid we had a fireplace and propane stove for heat. My brother installed a tiny solar panel to power a RV pump that pressurized our indoor plumbing. We had twelve-volt lights at night, a good well, a Servel propane refrigerator and a generator to boot.

Rocky had ten acres to play on, plus another fifty next door. Sometimes we kept horses for a family in town or boarded one or two temporarily. Several times I took my trailer over to the Nelson Livestock Auction and brought back a wild colt or filly to start and save them from certain death at the slaughterhouse. Rocky always had company of one sort or another and he was a good mentor to the younger ones, as a single mom with three kids I had my plate full.

I drove my poor old truck twelve hundred miles a month just to take

the kids to their school bus stop at the end of Coyote Springs Road. I had a decent home business that kept me busy, family close by, young colts to handle, and the kids with all their activities. Rocky was still my sanctuary. When I saddled up and rode out into the foothills all the stress in my life evaporated away and blew across the prairie like a tumbleweed. I was content. I loved living as far away from the city as I could. My children, horses, business and garden kept me occupied and I never felt lonely. I had become very independent and did not resemble the poor beaten down woman I used to be. Changing tires, splitting firewood, trenching with a pick ax, planting trees, building fence, carpentry and butchering were all part of my list of talents.

When my oldest daughter turned fifteen she decided to run for the Prescott Frontier Days Rodeo Queen's Court. It would be an interesting experience for all of us. She had one thing going for her that the other contestants didn't. She could ride. Really ride. At the age of five she had ridden her pony over a thousand miles at one time and became the second youngest member of the Long Riders Guild. While the other girls grew up riding in arenas or barrel racing my oldest was going the distance. She loved her horses and had a skill with them few could match. The horse she was to use for the events was injured part way through the contest and she ended up riding old Rocky. She rode him in all the Grand Entries at the rodeo and the parade. Rocky carried flags as she raced around the arena prior to each performance. Rocky pranced and bowed his neck and lived up to the Fire in his name. No one could tell by looking that her mount was in his twenties. For a horse that spent most of his life in the great outdoors he blended in quite well with all the other horses that were used to the commotion of the city.

In 1994 I remarried. With my previous experience having a man around the house I was very cautious. I was perfectly okay with the status quo and had come to the realization that man in my life was certainly not necessary for my survival. Righteous hard working men like my father just didn't exist anymore as far as I was concerned. And then God threw Bryon into my path.

We met on a blind date and had breakfast early one Saturday morning. The next time he came to visit he brought his Quarter Horse mare Sarah along and we went riding together. Unlike some of the men I had met, he didn't talk about a bad childhood or gossip badly about people

Previous page: Rocky at the Prescott Frontier Days Parade.

I didn't even know. He was intelligent and considerate. Bryon didn't live with his mother (BIG plus!) or use foul language. He opened doors for me. He didn't smell bad or reek of alcohol and his clothes were clean. Some of these things may seem trivial but they had become important to me and I looked him over with much scrutiny. Any red flags that popped up would have sent me fleeing.

`As we spent more time together it became obvious we were very like minded. Bryon was very polite and humble and he liked to create things. His talents were many. It seemed he could fix almost anything or build things from scratch if needed. I really must give his parents credit for a good upbringing. When Bryon sits down in front of a piano you can expect a musical treat even though he doesn't read music. But what astounded me the most was that when he took off his coat.....he put it on a hanger! I couldn't believe what I was seeing. I had heard about such rare occurrences but I never thought I'd actually see it happen. That clinched it for me. We became a couple.

I had asked God that in the event He had plans for me to remarry, to make sure that He brought me someone from the opposite side of the universe that the last one came from. He didn't disappoint.

Bryon in turn was accepting of the fact I was a woman with baggage. Three kids and about nineteen horses in the back yard. Not all the horses were mine. Some were boarders and some just passing through. Children grow up and begin lives of their own. But I made sure he understood there would always be a hayburner or two behind the house. Love me, love my horse. Take it or leave it. So far he's taken it well.

I had always wanted to have a horseback wedding. Bryon and I discussed it and came up with a plan that would be a unique event that our friends and families would enjoy.

We had Galen Neshem, whom I had met decades earlier at the Indian Rock Ranch do the service. He stood in my old doctor's buggy and read our vows. Bryon sat upon his mare Sarah and I sat atop old Rocky. A photographer from the Prescott Courier took pictures of the event and one of them ended up with the feature story on the front page of the newspaper the next morning. We served barbecue to our guests inside a Sioux Tipi, and had Tom Hyatt singing cowboy songs for our entertainment.

We bought the Turtle Rock Ranch soon afterwards and lived there the next five years. In 1999, we sold and moved lock, stock and business to Bagdad, Arizona. We ended up leasing the Byner Cattle

Riding Rocky at our wedding ceremony.

Company property from the Phelps Dodge Mining Corporation. The ranch consisted of several hundred acres just on the outskirts of town.

Rocky was in his thirties when we moved to the ranch. He was starting to show his age a little and I seldom rode him.

When we did go out it was only for a short while. Rocky had earned his retirement years. Several of his teeth were missing and he was having difficulty eating his alfalfa hay. He had a tendency to bind up so I switched him over to Equine Senior. In 2001 I saddled Rocky up and rode him down the main street of Bagdad in the Fourth of July Parade. He pranced sideways down the street as I waved at all my friends and neighbors. At the announcers stand we stopped and I informed him the horse I was riding was thirty-two years old. He had a hard time believing me and relayed the information to the crowd. I side-passed Rocky to the far side of the street and then we continued prancing to the finish.

While we lived in Bagdad I acquired a very nice APHA stallion named

Riding Rocky in the Burro Creek Canyon.

Boot Scootin and a few foundation bred mares. I had always wanted to raise quality APHA horses and the ranch we lived at had the facilities for it. Each spring Rocky had a new crop of foals to mentor. He would go out the gate into the enormous back pasture and follow the babies and their mothers up into the mountains behind the ranch.

On July 4th of 2004 Bryon and I left the ranch to drive the hour and thirty minutes to Prescott. I never was comfortable leaving the ranch with all the young foals running about. There were plenty of mountain lions in the area and horses, like kids can get into all kinds of trouble when you're not looking.

We made it as quick a trip as possible and arrived back around two in the afternoon. One of our mares, Pumpkin, had seriously damaged her leg a few weeks before. As soon as we arrived I counted the babies and scanned the mares. Then caught Pumpkin and put her in the wash rack to doctor her leg. It was very hot that afternoon and I spent extra time cooling her down with the hose. When I finally turned her loose I put her halter back on the wash rack and heard a noise behind me. I turned to see what had made the moaning sound and couldn't see where the noise had come from. The ground sloped down towards a creek just outside the arena gate and I heard the moan again. Walking quickly to the gate I could then see a horse laying flat on the ground. It was Rocky.

He was stuck. I reached him and touched his neck. Then ran back to the house to get Bryon. It would take two of us to get Rocky up. I had no idea how long he had lay there. He had laid down to roll on the piles of soft manure we had piled just outside the arena. The backside sloped down towards the dry creek bed and Rocky had managed to end up on that slope with his legs uphill. He could have rolled over to get up, but a huge old tree stump protruded out of the ground at his back. Bryon and I tried for a half-hour to move Rocky into a position where he could gain his footing. I brought buckets of water out and let Rocky drink. The sun was relentless. Finally Bryon went back to the house and called a friend from in town to help. We were both wearing ourselves out trying to pick up a thousand pounds of horse, and Rocky was weak and dehydrated. While Bryon was getting help I assessed the situation. The stump would have to be dug and or cut out so we could roll Rocky over and get his legs downhill.

With the help of the man from town we dug and pulled the dead stump out. I grabbed an extra lead rope and tied it to Rocky's hind foot. Then I came around to the downhill side and started to pull. Bryon pulled the lead attached to Rock's halter. The three of us were able to roll Rocky over. When Rocky realized he was in a different position he used all his strength to roll up on his knees where he could swallow more easily from the bucket. Then he laid his head back down. He was exhausted. We let him lay for a few minutes and then encouraged him to try to stand. I don't know if he was just weak, or if he had suffered a stroke or if his legs were just asleep from being still so long but it took several minutes of pulling and pushing and yelling to get him up. As he got his feet under him he stumbled next to a small tree and leaned against it for support. Rocky nickered a thanks once he found his footing. I let him rest in the sparse shade of the tree until he felt his strength return.

The next morning he seemed to have recovered from the incident and had returned back to his old geriatric self. He walked over to me and stood. I scratched his favorite fly bitten spot on his tummy and he held out his head at an angle in delight. He was much better. I rode him one more time that summer. Just around the ranch and always on the level. Rocky's knees were shaky now when he walked down any type on incline. I could feel the difference in how he moved compared to the horse he used to be. He was thirty-five years old and in good shape for his age but things were beginning to wear out. I didn't want to think about him coming to the point when he would die. All things did, but that was not my reality.

To me, Rocky would live forever, or I hoped at least into his forties. I could not accept the thought of life without him. We had been partners for thirty-two years.

Rocky at thirty-five, ears still pricked forward and always alert.

When summer vanished and the nights grew colder I would sometimes find Rocky still napping after the sun came up. He wasn't really asleep, his legs were just stiff from the night before and he needed a hand getting out of bed. I would call Bryon and we would put a halter on Rocky and with just a little help from us he could stand. Then Rocky would walk off to breakfast and spend the day around the mares and their half-grown babies. A couple weeks later he would need help again.

In November I was heading out to feed and Rocky fell in line behind me as I walked down the drive towards the barn. I heard a muffled humph behind me and turned to see Rocky down on the ground. I think he just missed stepped and fell off into the bar ditch, not coordinated or quick enough to catch himself. I called Bryon and grabbed Rocky's halter and we helped Rocky back onto his feet. Picking Rocky up after that seemed to happen more and more often. Each time it seemed we had to work harder and Rocky put in less effort.

One evening early in December I walked out to the corrals to feed and found Rocky lying down again. After feeding the other horses Bryon and I haltered Rocky and did our best to get him up. We called a friend out from town and the three of us spent a half-hour literally trying to lift a thousand pounds of horse from off the ground. Rocky finally got his front feet under him but the rear didn't follow. It was as if the back of him wasn't communicating with the front anymore. We gently let him lay back down and I put a couple of saddle blankets beneath his head. After dinner we walked out to see if there had been any change. There had not. Rocky had hardly moved. I asked my husband to give me some time alone with my horse so I could say good bye. I laid down across Rocky's neck and began to cry. I wrapped my fingers in his mane and stroked his cheek. I spent about an hour with him, then kissed him goodnight, knowing he would be gone before dawn. That night Bryon held me as I cried myself to sleep.

We woke at three-thirty in the morning and Bryon told me he would go check on Rocky to see if he had died. I prayed that he had. I didn't want my partner suffering out on the cold ground. Bryon came back to the house a few minutes later. I tried to read the expression on his face but I couldn't. "Is he gone?" I asked.

"No" was the reply.

The Bible has a verse in it about the tongue having the power of life or death. I never quite understood what that meant until that moment. I had to authorize the death of my beloved Rocky. I knew Bryon wouldn't do it unless I asked him too. Our closest vet was over eighty miles away and I knew him well enough to know that he would not come out in the middle of the night to put down an old horse. At least not one that was eighty miles away. I wanted Rocky's suffering and pain to stop. Bryon knelt down in front of me and looked into my wet eyes. "Honey, you know what needs to be done. Tell me what you want me to do."

Rocky's body was shutting down but his great heart refused to give up. I couldn't do this to my friend. I couldn't let him suffer. I looked up at Bryon and said, "Put him down."

Bryon walked into our office and came out trying to hide the holstered gun from me. Then closed the door quietly behind him and left. I picked up a pillow from the sofa next to me and began screaming into it. I screamed at the top of my lungs uncontrollably till my voice went raw. I had never felt such grief. Part of me was dying and I cried out from the anguish.

My father had died a few years earlier and I did not feel this pain. I loved my daddy dearly and cried at his passing but not like this. Likewise with my mother. I was sad and cried when she died.

My connection to Rocky was stronger than that of my parents. Were Rocky and my spirits so entwined that at his death the pain of them separating was unbearable? I don't know. We had been through so much together it was going to be difficult for me to adjust to a world without him.

The next morning I had to spend the day at a local arts event. I asked Bryon to feed so I wouldn't have to walk past where Rocky lay even though Bryon had covered him with a tarp. Bryon made arrangements while I was gone and had a backhoe come out. Rocky was buried there on the ranch in Bagdad near a grove of cottonwood trees. It was weeks before I could walk near his grave. Just looking in its direction made me cry.

The next few months brought new foals to distract me but I could feel a deep hole left behind as I scanned the corrals for a horse that was no longer there.

Rocky had lived to an age most horses never see. The majority of horses live being passed around from owner to owner, getting used and abused along the way. Very few are kept for their entire lives. Each of them has a history that could be told. I was just fortunate to be there to witness and be a part of the life story of an amazing little ranch horse named Rocky Fire.

Rocky Fire and Sunny living the good life at Turtle Rock Ranch, Coyote Springs.

I'll lend you for a little while
My grandest foal He said.
For you to love while he's alive
And morn for when he's dead.

It may be one or twenty years,
Or days or months, you see.
But will you, till I take him back
Take care of him for me?

He'll bring his charms to gladden you,
And should his stay be brief
You'll have treasured memories
As solace for your grief.

I can not promise he will stay,
Since all from earth return.
But there are lessons taught on earth
I want this foal to learn.

I've looked the wide world over
In my search for teachers true.
And from the throngs that crowd life's lanes, with trust I have selected you.

Now will you give him your total love?
Nor think the labor vain,
Nor hate me when I come
To take him back again?

I know you'll give him tenderness
And love will bloom each day.
And for the happiness you've known
Forever grateful stay.

But should I come and call for him
Much sooner than you've planned
You'll brave the bitter grief that comes
And someday you'll understand.

Author: Unknown

Comments from the author

From time to time I get asked the question "Did you ever get a replacement for Rocky?" I have to answer "No". Have I had other horses? Yes. Rocky is irreplaceable. Each horse is an individual. They have as many personalities as people. It's a lucky person indeed to have a true friend that lasts a lifetime. People, like horses, come and go throughout our lives. Some hang around more than others. Very few hang around until the end. As you have read, Rocky was a lifeline for me through some very hard times. And like a true companion, we also shared the best adventures.

When I bought Rocky in 1972 I wasn't expecting to have him for the next thirty-two years. Although Rocky had some serious issues at the start we worked them out as a team and built on that relationship to form a bond that lasted a lifetime.

I have been fortunate to have several outstanding horses over the years although none could hold the place in my heart I have for Rocky. If God has a place in heaven for horses, I hope Dale will keep the 'rough' off Rocky till I get there.

40072324R00061

Made in the USA
San Bernardino, CA
10 October 2016